The Catechism of the Catholic Church
and the Craft of Catechesis

The Catechism of the Catholic Church
and the Craft of Catechesis

by

Pierre de Cointet, Barbara Morgan, and Petroc Willey

With an introductory essay by
Christoph Cardinal Schönborn

IGNATIUS PRESS   SAN FRANCISCO

Cover icon: *Christ the Teacher II*, by Brother Claude Lane, O.S.B.

Cover design by Riz Boncan Marsella

© 2008 by Ignatius Press, San Francisco
All rights reserved
ISBN 978-1-58617-221-3
Library of Congress Control Number 2007928633
Printed in the United States of America ∞

To every catechist

"The taste and tincture of another education"
— *Thomas Traherne*

Contents

Preface

In the fullness of time, God revealed himself and his loving plan of salvation in his beloved Son, through the power of the Holy Spirit. God came and dwelt among us, full of grace and truth. The Father *teaches us by coming among us*, in his Son and Spirit. God's revelation and the manner of its transmission cannot be separated. And in the fullness of time, God's desire for embodiment received its perfect response:

> [G]iving her consent to God's word, Mary becomes the mother of Jesus. Espousing the divine will for salvation wholeheartedly, without a single sin to restrain her, she gave herself entirely to the person and to the work of her Son; she did so in order to serve the mystery of redemption with him and dependent on him, by God's grace.[1]

In this revelation of the condescension, mercy and faithfulness of God, and in the perfection of Mary's response, we see the whole of the craft of catechesis. We see what the Church has called the "pedagogy of God". God has his own way of teaching. And in this way, this pedagogy, which we are invited to learn, God reveals *what* we are to teach, how we are to *receive* this teaching, and how we are to participate, under God's grace, in its *transmission*.

The underlying thesis and conviction of this small book, then, is that the *Catechism of the Catholic Church* not only offers us a new, definitive account for our time of the contents of the Catholic Faith; *its value for the catechist lies more broadly in the pedagogy that informs every page*. Those participating in the teaching mission of the Church can learn from the *Catechism* not only what *is* the Deposit of Faith but also *how to receive and to hand on* that deposit in a truly ecclesial way. Appreciating this pedagogy enables us to practice catechesis as a *craft* in which content and the methods of transmission are united in a living whole: we are apprenticed into the Lord's own school of

---

[1] *Catechism of the Catholic Church*, 494; this source hereafter abbreviated CCC; cf. LG 56.

learning and teaching. For this is how the Lord teaches, we believe, as act and word together and, amazingly, as Word made historical flesh.

The *Catechism* is rightly understood to be, in the first place, an annunciation, a proclamation, of the Faith of the Church for our day. It is a presentation of the "essential" and "fundamental" points of the Faith (see CCC 11). Every Catholic can refer to the *Catechism* to gain a secure understanding of the Church's teaching on matters of faith and morals. For catechists, then, the *Catechism* is the key reference work for their teaching, the utterly reliable place to which they can turn. Approved by the bishops of the whole Church, the *Catechism* is a uniquely collaborative work, drawing on the wisdom and insights of Catholics from every culture. It is a work for teaching all nations that has involved the bishops of every nation in its compilation and writing.

It is less well known and appreciated that the *Catechism of the Catholic Church* is also a superbly crafted work from which *to learn* and *to teach*. The teaching follows from the learning, for as one learns from the *Catechism* one gains not only a deepening understanding of God's gratuitous plan for our salvation, but also a sense of growing wonder at the learning process itself, as one's heart and mind are enlarged to welcome and receive these truths in one's own life. The *Catechism* is utterly faithful to the truth that God's revelation *is* his very act of transmission, his gift of himself to us. And we are invited into that truth, to hand ourselves over to it (see Rom 6:17), so that we can ourselves hand on the Faith to others. And it is from this love of learning from, and with, the Lord that the catechist is able to discover in his own life a growing love for God's revelation of himself in Christ, for the process of learning and transmission, and for the learner. The introduction to the *Compendium of the Catechism of the Catholic Church* points us precisely to this pedagogical dimension of the *Catechism*, speaking of the "wisdom of its presentation":

> In fact, the *Compendium* is meant to reawaken interest in and enthusiasm for the *Catechism*, which, in the wisdom of its presentation and the depth of its spirituality, always remains the basic text for catechesis in the Church today.[2]

---

[2] Joseph Cardinal Ratzinger, "Introduction", in *Compendium of the Catechism of the Catholic Church* (London: Catholic Truth Society, 2006), no. 3.

For these reasons, the *Catechism* is not a work to be read briefly or hastily; one needs to stay with the text, pray with it and immerse oneself in it to appreciate fully its visionary power and the compelling sense of beauty, goodness, and truth that radiates from its pages. In these pages we meet the Spirit at work in his Church. The *Catechism* is a place of "personal encounter" (see CCC 2563), and it is in and through this encounter that a truly Spirit-led pedagogy can emerge and inspire one's teaching methods, a pedagogy flowing directly from one's prayerful understanding of the Faith. It is in and through this encounter that the authentic craft of catechesis can arise.

To read the *Catechism* in this way, searching its depths and allowing oneself to be questioned and challenged by it in order to teach effectively from it, one needs to understand some of the elements that structure and inform its pedagogy of the Faith. When these elements are firmly grasped and their significance appreciated the *Catechism* can become one of the most transforming and penetrating teaching tools the Church has ever possessed.

It is no small thing to be, as the *Catechism* is, an excellent instrument for both learning *and* teaching, just as it is no small thing to be oneself both a learner and a teacher. This requires the drawing together of the contemplative and the active dimensions of our lives, the uniting of the two.[3]

A learner must be able to contemplate things as they are; a book to assist learning must help in this. It must assist in a contemplative attitude toward things, enabling the mind to grasp them as they are. This the *Catechism* does par excellence. It is structured, organized, and written to support a deeply contemplative appreciation of the doctrines of the Faith. It offers us an unveiling of the meaning of doctrine through the twin avenues of reasoning and the focus of a "humbly attentive heart" (CCC 2668), "a *gaze* of faith" (CCC 2715). On the one hand, the *Catechism* asks the mind to engage actively with the annunciation of the Faith, following its tight, reasoned presentation of doctrine. On the other hand, it invites a mode of learning of the Faith not unlike that of *lectio divina*. In *lectio divina*, or "divine reading", the scriptures are read slowly and attentively, the mind resting on the words and

---

[3] On this see Josef Pieper, *Guide to Thomas Aquinas* (San Francisco: Ignatius Press, 1991), pp. 93–97.

phrases in a way that has been described as a little like a cow cud-
ding.[4] The *Catechism* benefits from this slow reading aloud of its text,
this pondering of its meaning, of its precise, taut, yet contemplative
text.

A good teacher also needs to see things with the eyes of the one he
is teaching, thereby needing to focus on the vision that the learner
will have of the subject. A book, if it is to assist in the craft of teaching, must facilitate this work of the teacher as well. The *Catechism*
achieves this too. As well as emphasizing the necessary distinctions
among learners that the teacher needs to bear in mind (see CCC 24),
it adopts a structure and organization that enable the teacher always to
begin with what is small, individual, the beginning point in understanding and study, so as to move on from there to what is greater and
perhaps harder to grasp. The writing of the *Catechism* text in short,
numbered paragraphs is an example and a practical outworking of this
intention. It also adopts a style that enables one to enter into each
subject with the fresh awareness of one approaching it for the first
time. The *Catechism* employs a gracious and classical style, straightforward, precise, and elegant. The text communicates a reverence and
love for the subjects with which it is dealing, drawing the reader into
a simple and direct relationship with the various doctrines, and in and
through these doctrines to a deepening adherence to the Person of
Christ.

The present book, then, aims to bring to light the pedagogy embedded in the *Catechism*, setting out the principles and steps for putting
this pedagogy into practice. It explains very simply how every catechist can discover the key principles that enable one to *learn from*
and *teach from* the *Catechism*, so that we are nourished and enriched
by our Mother, the Church, even as we teach. Chapter by chapter,
this book builds up a full picture of this pedagogy, explaining the
catechetical "keys", making clear why they are of such importance,
and illustrating them with numerous examples. In this way, it aims
to help catechists to see how the *Catechism* may be used directly as
the basic resource for catechetical work and as the reference point
for planning and teaching.

---

[4] See André Louf, *Teach Us to Pray* (London: Darton, Longman and Todd, 1974), pp. 46–
47, and see Ezek 3:1–13.

On a practical level, the book helps catechists to see how the *Catechism* identifies key teaching points for any subject and how to immerse one's catechesis in the living, ecclesial sources of the Faith, so that catechetical sessions are occasions for a deepening attachment to Christ, who is revealed and handed on to us in the Church's Tradition, Sacred Scriptures, and liturgy. Above all, the book follows the *Catechism* in highlighting the inseparability of the delivery of catechesis from the person and prayer of the catechist: as a work of the Church, catechetics is rooted in the incarnational reality of the Word becoming flesh—becoming flesh in the person of the catechist and becoming flesh in those to whom catechesis is delivered.

This little book, then, is both a manual for practical use and an invitation to seek and to find a renewal of one's spiritual life through the ministry of catechesis, in which the catechist can gratefully draw, in prayer, on the life, gifts, and interior guidance of the Holy Spirit. The *Catechism* offers us the possibility of discovering an "organic connection" between the spiritual life and dogma as the secret for the renewal of both catechesis and spirituality, both being avenues toward the One who is all-good, all-true, and all-beautiful.

A pedagogy of the Faith

That the Faith has its own specific pedagogy may perhaps be a new idea for us. The *General Directory for Catechesis*, however, calls upon catechists to consider "the demands" and "the originality" of "that pedagogy which is proper to the faith" (no. 31; this source hereafter abbreviated GDC). The Church has certain "demands", or requirements, with regard to pedagogy. She has expectations not only concerning the content of what we teach, but also how we teach it. This is the case because the Faith generates its own pedagogy. The Faith is inseparable from pedagogy, the pedagogy of God, and our catechesis is to follow this pedagogy. To discover such a pedagogy is not to uncover a single or restrictive methodology—we need to distinguish carefully here between a *method of teaching* on the one hand and the *pedagogy of God* on the other. By method we mean a specific way of organizing and structuring one's teaching so as to bring about learning. This book is not directly about such methods of teaching; it concerns God's pedagogy, which is something much more all-encompassing. In fact, this pedagogy is informed by a *largesse* that can welcome every authentic and creative teaching style.

The *Directory* also says that the pedagogy we are invited to follow is an *original* one. The word "original" signals two connected things here. In the first place, there is something *unique* about the content of the Faith. Pope John Paul II often wrote about the sense of wonder and amazement that we have as we contemplate the Faith we have received. In the second place, the word "original" indicates that the uniqueness of the Faith is intrinsically *related to its origin*. The Faith is not generated out of human experience, whether individual or collective. It is not simply the result even of the accumulation of centuries of human wisdom and analysis. It is not the creation of man. It is given from God (see CCC 51).

When describing the word "pedagogy", then, "original" does not simply mean "unusual"; it also means a pedagogy rooted in the *origins* of the Faith. We turn to the sources of the Faith and the media of revelation to discover it. John Paul's introduction to the *Catechism* clarifies this point when he speaks of the *Catechism* offering us a "catechesis renewed at the living sources of the faith"[5].

The pedagogy we shall be exploring in this book is one that is derived from the Faith of the Church and follows the content and contours of that Faith. The *Catechism*, as a work of collaboration between the Holy Spirit and the successors to the apostles, is written with this divine pedagogy flowing through it. The heart of the Deposit of Faith, its center, lies in the revelation of the Heart of God in the Person of Jesus Christ (see CCC 478, 609). The pedagogy of God, therefore, has its culminating point in the appearing among us of the Savior, Jesus, the one in whom we find our happiness, the fullness of truth, and our way of return to the Father. We shall see that catechesis is conceived by the *Catechism* to be the annunciation of this and the invitation to participate in the *fiat* of Mary, in the paschal grace and work of an ever-deepening conversion and conforming of our lives to the image of the Son in his Bride, the Church.

This book is written for all those involved in the work of catechesis in the Church, whether this takes place in the parish, the home, or

---

[5] John Paul II, Apostolic Constitution *Fidei Depositum*, p. 3 (October 11, 1997); this source hereafter abbreviated FD.

the school. It is offered to bishops and to those to whom they delegate responsibility for catechesis at the diocesan level. It is offered to priests, and to those religious and laity working in collaboration with them. It is also intended to be of assistance to parents, the principal educators of their children in the home.

This work does not offer a history of catechetics, nor does it see its focus as lying in discussions of current debates in catechetics. Nonetheless, both of these aspects are relevant to the presentation of catechetics outlined here. On the whole, however, the reader will find both the historical and the more discursive elements in the footnotes. This leaves the main text free to develop the exposition of the pedagogy of God, drawing on Scripture and Tradition and guided by the texts of the Magisterium.

The book begins with an essay by Christoph Cardinal Schönborn on the Church's mandate to teach, a mission from which we may draw strength and grace. An appreciation of this point lies at the heart of all endeavors to participate fruitfully in the pedagogy of God. The first chapter follows, setting forth the foundations for developing the craft of catechesis using the *Catechism*. The pedagogy of God, especially as it is revealed to us in the *Catechism*, is then explored in seven further ways, each way offering us pedagogical "keys" for our learning and teaching. Through these chapters, then, the meaning of the most important terms in this pedagogy are systematically unpacked and their catechetical implications uncovered. We hope that readers are led to see the beauty, necessity, and practicality of the catechetical principles that are presented both explicitly and implicitly in the *Catechism*. The focus of the final chapter turns more explicitly to the life of the catechist: the significance of the theological virtues for the life of the catechist is uncovered, as well as their pedagogical importance, and the place of the spiritual gifts and the life of prayer crowns the book.

Acknowledgments

This book is the result of friendships and collaborations, quietly maturing over a number of years, between many people engaged in the catechetical work of the Church. Here we gratefully acknowledge the "amicitia catechistica" of those working at, or attached to, the Office of Catechetics at Franciscan University, Steubenville; the Studium of Notre-Dame de Vie in Venasque; and the Maryvale Institute in England. In addition, we would like particularly to acknowledge the inspiration provided by two remarkable groups and signs of hope for catechetics in the Church: the Association for Catechumenal Ministry and the Bethlehem Community in North Dakota.

To Christoph Cardinal Schönborn we owe an enormous debt, both for his editing of the *Catechism of the Catholic Church*—surely the single most important contribution to the work of catechetics in the Church since the apostolic age—and for his personal encouragement of this project and of our collaboration.

Abbreviations

CCC   *Catechism of the Catholic Church*, second edition (© 1997)

CT   *Catechesi tradendae*

DS   Denzinger–Schönmetzer, *Enchiridion symbolorum* (1965)

DV   *Dei Verbum*

FR   *Fides et ratio*

FD   *Fidei Depositum*

GDC   *General Directory for Catechesis*

GCD   *General Catechetical Directory*

GS   *Gaudium et Spes*

HV   *Humanae vitae*

LG   *Lumen gentium*

PG   Migne, *Patrologia graeca*

PL   Migne, *Patrologia latina*

RM   *Redemptoris Missio*

SC   *Sacrosanctum concilium*

SCG   *Summa contra gentiles*

SRS   *Sollicitudo rei socialis*

ST   *Summa theologica*

UR   *Unitatis redintegratio*

Information on many of these sources is provided in the "Index of Citations" found in the back of the *Catechism of the Catholic Church*.

Introduction
By Whose Authority?

By whose authority is the *Catechism of the Catholic Church* offered to us? And what is the *nature and character* of that authority? Before turning to the *Catechism of the Catholic Church* and to the Church's Magisterium for guidance for catechesis, as we do in this book, it is important to consider how the Church understands her authority from Christ to proclaim the Deposit of Faith as true for all people and all time. We will find, I think, that there are many unexpected aspects of the authority of the Church of which we can become aware, the understanding of which can enable us to embrace such authority in free and loving obedience. Certainly, it is only by clarifying the meaning that the Church attaches to her authority to teach that we can move forward in our understanding of the role of the *Catechism* for the work of catechesis.

An authority to "abide by"

We are members of a Church that speaks and acts authoritatively because Jesus did. The crowds "were astonished at his teaching, for he taught them as one who had authority, and not as their scribes" (Mt 7:28–29). Jesus was recognized as different from other religious teachers, and one of the differences lay in the authority with which he spoke and acted. The Magisterium of the Catholic Church is also recognized as distinctive, and part of this distinctiveness lies, as for Christ, in the authority with which the Church speaks.

Clearly, then, we need to examine our understanding of the authority of the Church and also our relationship to it. Accepting an authority is never a step to be taken lightly because it entails an "obedience" to, an "abiding by", the words of another. Naturally, we want to obey, or abide by, only an authority that is thoroughly concerned for our good.

We often hear it said that one must "abide by the rules". The term "abiding" also suggests something else: staying in a safe place; resting peacefully; remaining where we wish to be, in a place in which our good is securely held. The *Catechism* makes it clear that the authority of the Church exists ultimately for the sake of leading us to a state of "abiding", to a place of rest, safe, permanent, and peaceful. This image is highlighted in the *Catechism*, in the section that speaks of eternal beatitude (see CCC 1720), and our attention is drawn to the Letter to the Hebrews, which speaks of a "sabbath rest" awaiting the people of God who obey the Lord's voice (Heb 4:9–10). St. Augustine concludes his *City of God* with a description of the delights of "entering into" and "abiding" in this rest: "There we shall rest and see, we shall see and love, we shall love and praise. Behold what will be at the end without end. For what other end do we have, if not to reach the kingdom which has no end?" (22:30, 5).

The link between "authority" and "abiding" is also indicated in the design of the logo on the cover of the *Catechism of the Catholic Church*. There we see the image of the Good Shepherd, who is described as the one who "leads and protects his faithful (the lamb) by his authority (the staff), draws them by the symphony of the truth (the panpipes), and makes them lie down in the shade of the tree of life, his redeeming Cross which opens paradise" (CCC, p. ii).

The purpose of the authority of the Good Shepherd is to enable the sheep to "lie down" beneath the tree of life, so that paradise might be made available for them. The authority of the Good Shepherd is one that *leads* to safety and away from danger, and an authority that *protects*—protects the good and protects from harm. It is also an authority to play the symphony of the Faith, an authority of proclaiming and interpreting truth. The *Catechism* speaks of this aspect of authority when it declares that "the pastoral duty of the Magisterium is aimed at seeing to it that the People of God *abides* in the truth that liberates" (CCC 890, emphasis added). Jesus, who is the Truth, called his disciples to "abide" in him: "Abide in me, and I in you" (see Jn 15:4), and we do so through believing in him and participating in our Eucharistic communion with him (see Jn 6:40, 56). The Church's authority is for the sake of enabling us to abide in Christ, our whole spiritual good (see CCC 1324).

This truth that liberates and that the Church must never cease to proclaim is found in the Cross of Christ, the tree of life. It is by virtue of Christ's sacrifice on this tree that sin is overcome so that we may lie down in its "shade". And the *Catechism* reminds us that this "event of the Cross and Resurrection *abides* and draws everything toward life" (CCC 1085). The redeeming Cross of Christ "opens paradise". The opening of paradise for the whole of mankind, then, is the only purpose of authority: paradise to which the love of the Father, the mission of Christ, and the power of the Holy Spirit are to draw and gather us, through their authority handed over into the Church.

An authority "under authority"

Every exercise of authority in the Church is a service; every exercise of authority is also an expression of power. Both of these are the case by virtue of the fact that her authority is exercised on behalf of another—of Christ—in whom power and service were perfectly united.

> The sacrament of Holy Orders communicates a "sacred power" which is none other than that of Christ. The exercise of this authority must therefore be measured against the model of Christ, who by love made himself the least and the servant of all (cf. Mk 10:43–45; 1 Pet 5:3).[1]

The authority of the Church, then, is not her own, but that of Christ. And we can remember that Christ, too, spoke of his authority as received from another, from his Father: "I do nothing on my own authority but speak thus as the Father taught me" (Jn 8:28). Jesus Christ, although he is the Son by nature, describes himself as a servant (Mk 10:42–45): a servant belongs to another. His time and energy are not his own. The source of the Son's authority lies in his belonging entirely to his Father.

The centurion whose servant was healed by Jesus recognizes the importance, for the exercise of authority, of being under authority oneself: "For I am a man *under authority*, with soldiers *under me*; and I say to one, 'Go,' and he goes, and to another, 'Come,' and he comes, and to my slave, 'Do this,' and he does it."[2]

When the Lord saw that he responded in this way he "marveled": "Not even in Israel have I found such faith" (Mt 8:10). As we have seen, the Son is himself under authority: he does only what the Father

---

[1] CCC 1551.
[2] Mt 8:9; emphases added; see also Lk 7:8.

bids him do, and he speaks only what the Father bids him speak. This is the truth that liberated him, so that the crowds marveled at the authority with which he spoke and acted (see Mk 1:27). Liberated through being under the Father's authority, he was free to speak and act with that authority.

The Church is also "under authority". She does only what the Son and the Spirit assist her in doing (see CCC 85–87). Being "under authority" the Church places herself among the least; the Pope himself is known as the "servant of the servants of God". Holding authority "under authority" is the only way to understand this reality within the Church. Being "under authority", the Magisterium can only exercise the authority that it has itself received, that of God the Father, in Jesus Christ, by the power of the Holy Spirit. It does not have any other. And because of this, the Church, too, is free to speak and act with that same authority.

The authority of the Church is rooted in the Father's love. The Church's authority to teach is an authority grounded wholly in the loving purpose of the Father. The *Catechism* reminds us: "Through Jeremiah, God declares to his people, 'I have loved you with an everlasting love; therefore I have continued my faithfulness to you'" (CCC 220, citing Jer 31:3). It explains further, "God himself is an eternal exchange of love, Father, Son, and Holy Spirit, and he has destined us to share in that exchange" (CCC 221). The plan of God's loving kindness is continued in the Church (see CCC 257), which is why the "whole concern of doctrine" must be directed to this same love.[3]

The authority of the Church is also a participation in the Son's mission from the Father. The authority which Jesus Christ gave to his apostles, upon whom he founded his Church, is the authority which he himself had received from his Father.

> All authority in heaven and on earth has been given to me. Go therefore and make disciples of all nations, baptizing them in the name of the Father and of the Son and of the Holy Spirit, teaching them to observe all that I have commanded you; and behold, I am with you always, to the close of the age.[4]

Jesus handed over his mission and his authority to the apostles from his Father: "As the Father has sent me, even so I send you" (Jn 20:21).

[3] CCC 25; citing *Roman Catechism*, Preface 10; cf. 1 Cor 13:8.
[4] Mt 28:19–20.

And in handing over this authority, he does not leave them: he co-missions them. He chooses that he and they should continue the mission of the Father together, in dependence on the Holy Spirit, who empties his life into the Church so that she may be filled with the Spirit's grace and power (see GDC 37, 43). Jesus had prepared his disciples, during the three years of their common life, to join him in his mission, and he had promised to Peter the keys of the kingdom, calling him the rock upon whom he would build his Church (see Mt 16:16–20). "Thus the Church's mission is not an addition to that of Christ and the Holy Spirit, but is its sacrament" (CCC 738).

The authority of the Church draws from the power of the Holy Spirit. Before his Passover, Jesus announced that he would ask the Father to send to the disciples "another Counselor to be with you for ever, even the Spirit of truth, whom the world cannot receive, because it neither sees him nor knows him; you know him, for he dwells with you, and will be in you." [5]

On Easter-day this promise was fulfilled, as the Risen Lord appeared to the disciples and breathed on them: "Receive the Holy Spirit. If you forgive the sins of any, they are forgiven; if you retain the sins of any, they are retained" (Jn 20:22–23). And when the seven weeks of Easter had come to an end, the triumph of Christ's Passover was handed on through the outpouring of the Holy Spirit at Pentecost (see Acts 2:1–4 and CCC 731). Therefore, the Holy Spirit is the "principal agent of the whole of the Church's mission" (CCC 852, citing RM 21), guiding the Church in her growing understanding of the heritage of the Faith (CCC 94) so that it may be available for the salvation of all.

Finally, the authority of the Church is also an authority of the apostles. The successors to the apostles, the bishops, are "under" the authority of the original "foundations" of the Church. In John's vision of the Heavenly City he sees that there are not only twelve foundations for the wall of the city, with the names of the twelve apostles on the foundations (see Rev 21:14), but also that the tree of life bears "twelve kinds of fruit" (Rev 22:2). The apostles remain *fruitful* in the Church. Christ handed on his mission to these twelve apostles, and their successors receive their authority "through" that of the apostles. "Christ, whom the Father hallowed and sent into the world, has, through his

[5] Jn 14:16–17.

apostles, made their successors, the bishops namely, sharers in his consecration and mission."[6]

In the Second Letter to Timothy and in the Letter to Titus we have examples of the responsibility to teach that was passed on by the apostles to their successors. St. Paul writes to his "son" Timothy:

> I remind you to rekindle the gift of God that is within you through the laying on of my hands.... Follow the pattern of the sound words which you have heard from me, in the faith and love which are in Christ Jesus; guard the truth that has been entrusted to you by the Holy Spirit who dwells within us.[7]

And he continues:

> I charge you in the presence of God and of Christ Jesus who is to judge the living and the dead, and by his appearing and his kingdom: preach the word, be urgent in season and out of season, convince, rebuke, and exhort, be unfailing in patience and in teaching.... [A]lways be steady, endure suffering, do the work of an evangelist, fulfil your ministry.[8]

And to his other "son", Titus, in the apostolate, he writes likewise: "Show yourself in all respects a model of good deeds, and in your teaching show integrity, gravity, and sound speech that cannot be censured, so that an opponent may be put to shame, having nothing evil to say.... [E]xhort and reprove with all authority.[9]

The authority of the mission of Jesus Christ

Any participation in Christ's mission also needs to be considered in relation to his threefold ministry of priest, prophet, and king (LG 21). We can examine the Church's authority, therefore, in this same light.

The authority and service of Christ the King

We saw earlier that the logo selected for the cover of the *Catechism* presented the authority of the Good Shepherd as being at the service of *leading* and *protecting* the flock.

---

[6] LG 28. This is cited in CCC 1562.
[7] 2 Tim 1:6, 13.
[8] 2 Tim 4:1–2, 5.
[9] Tit 2:7–8, 15.

Let us consider first how the Good Shepherd *leads* his "little flock" (Lk 12:32). "Authority" derives from the Latin word *auctor*, which means "increase", "augment", and "promote" as well as "originate". We have here, then, an understanding of "authority" as being at the service of the work of building up and increasing the mission of the Church, assisting in her healthy growth and fruitfulness. The *Catechism* speaks of the "apostolic fruitfulness" (CCC 1550) of the Church, and it calls the ministerial priesthood "a *means* by which Christ unceasingly *builds up* and *leads* his Church" (CCC 1547; emphasis added). We can be confident that, with "the assistance of the Holy Spirit, the understanding of both the realities and the words of the heritage of faith is able to grow in the life of the Church" (CCC 94). This "leading" of the People of God culminates, through the redeeming grace of God, in their entry into paradise, and the flock is led to lie down in the shade of the tree of life since "apart from the cross there is no other ladder by which we may get to heaven." [10]

"Authority" also has to do with origins. Here, the Church's apostolic authority *protects* the truth of the origins and of the Author of the revelation she treasures. The revelation she offers comes "from above" (Jn 3:31). The Church's message of mercy is born, as she herself is born, in the "Father's heart" (CCC 758). The Church's authority protects the essential truth that "there is another order of knowledge, which man cannot possibly arrive at by his own powers: the order of divine Revelation" (CCC 50). "We do not think up faith on our own. It does not come *from* us as an idea of ours but *to* us as a word from outside." [11]

This protection of revelation, of the truth that is given "from above", is inseparable from the Church's protection of the full truth concerning the human person. The *Catechism* quotes from St. Ambrose, who exclaims, "O man, you did not dare to raise your face to heaven, you lowered your eyes to the earth, and suddenly you have received the grace of Christ" (CCC 2783). [12] What is at stake, then, is also the dignity of the human person, "whose defence and promotion have

---

[10] St. Rose of Lima: cf. P. Hanson, *Vita mirabilis* (Louvain, 1668). This is cited in CCC 618.

[11] Joseph Ratzinger, *Gospel, Catechesis, Catechism* (San Francisco: Ignatius Press, 1997), p. 30.

[12] The *Catechism* is citing from *De Sacramentis* 5, 4, 19; PL 16:450–51.

been entrusted to us by the Creator" (SRS 47). The protection of the Deposit of Faith and the truth of revelation is at the same time the safeguard for man's understanding of his true dignity as a child of the Father, "called to beatitude" (CCC 1949).

The authority and service of Christ the High Priest

We have already seen that Christ's "authority" is in fact a way of speaking about his whole-hearted handing over of himself to the authority of the Father's will, so that he might embrace God's benevolent plan by laying down his life in sacrifice for us. The authority that he gave to his apostles, therefore, on the day before his redeeming sacrifice on Calvary, was the authority to celebrate the Holy Eucharist, commanding them to do this in remembrance of him (see Lk 22:14–20). He hands over to his apostles the authority to offer his saving sacrifice.

The apostles are called to bring the fruits of the Paschal mystery to the whole world by guarding and transmitting the Deposit of Faith through teaching, and also by dispensing this deposit of grace through the liturgy. When Christ commissions the apostles after his resurrection, he tells them not only to *teach* "all that I have commanded you" but also to "*Baptize* . . ." (see Mt 28:18–20). The truth about God and his plan for us is to be communicated to us both through teaching and through Christ's sacrifice, in which we participate through the sacraments. The mystery of Christ is thus for us inseparably a Deposit of Faith and a "deposit of grace", offering us communion with the Savior of the world.

The Church lives by the power of Christ's authoritative sacrifice: it is a sacrifice that can touch sin and redeem man from sin's power, but cannot itself be touched *by* sin. There is something important to realize here concerning the weaknesses, the sins, the prejudices, the shortcomings, and the blindness in Christ's ministers, in those endowed with Christ's own authority but not yet conformed to his purity of life. The authority of the Church *can* be trusted in her ministers, the bishops and priests, as the authority of Christ. Therefore, this authority belongs to another "order" than that of human failure—or, sometimes, even of deep sin. This fact is particularly manifested in the Church's understanding of the sacraments, which are "not wrought by the righteousness of either the celebrant or the recipient, but by the power of God".[13] "This is the meaning of the Church's affirmation that the sacraments act *ex opere operato* (literally: 'by the very fact of the action's being performed')" (CCC 1128).[14] The sacraments are effective because "in them Christ himself is at work: ... it is he who acts in his sacraments in order to communicate the grace that each sacrament signifies" (CCC 1127). This is the beauty of God's plan of communicating his way, his truth, and his life: the divine authority given to the successors of the apostles in the Church is the authority to conserve and transmit the Deposit of Faith and to communicate the life of Christ through the sacraments, in each case integrally and purely as the work of God (see CCC 85–87, 100, 774).

The authority and service of Christ as Prophet

Being under authority has an unexpected effect: people were amazed at Christ's way of speaking with authority, with clarity, conviction, and a humble boldness; and this is how the apostles learnt to speak from Christ, with the Holy Spirit working in them. This is also how the Church continues to speak, not being anxious since she speaks with the authority of Christ and the Holy Spirit (see Lk 10:16; Mk 13:10–12).

The apostles were provided with helpers in their mission to preach and teach the faith. Some of these were what we can call the "first catechists". In his Letters, St. Paul speaks of them as his very dear and faithful helpers in the work of the Lord. Some may have been future successors of the apostles in the episcopate and priesthood, such as Timothy (see Rom 16:21; 1 Cor 16:10; Phil 2:19); others were deacons or lay people. They were united with the apostle in learning, protecting, and teaching the truth of the gospel with integrity and fidelity. Through their preaching and teaching of God's Word, the ministers of the Word enabled these catechists, and all those in their care, to abide in the truth. It is this abiding in the truth that confers freedom, as Jesus promised: "If you continue [abide] in my word, you are truly my disciples, and you will know the truth, and the truth will make you free" (Jn 8:31–32).

Catechists, then, are those who know that they can find true freedom through abiding in the Word that they receive from the Church.

---

[13] St. Thomas Aquinas, *ST* III, 68, 8 (also cited in CCC 1128).
[14] Cf. Council of Trent (1547): DS 1608.

They have accepted the invitation to suffer "the loss of all things" in order to seek and find the "surpassing worth of knowing Christ Jesus" (Phil 3:8; cited in CCC 428), through handing themselves over in the Church to the authoritative protection and guidance they receive there. The handing on of the Faith can take place fruitfully only when one has already offered one's whole being to the Lord, "to be wholly God's, because he is wholly ours" (CCC 2617). Catechists are those who, realizing the riches of grace (Eph 1:7) that have been poured out on the world through Christ, hand themselves over wholeheartedly and without reserve, to faithfully teach Christ and his message to others, thereby serving "the mystery of redemption with him and dependent on him, by God's grace" (CCC 494; cf. LG 56).

The truth that we have been called to teach is the one and divine revealed truth entrusted to the Church, and the authority we have to teach this truth is valid to the extent that we are "handed over into" the authoritative teaching office of the Church, the Magisterium. In this way, "[e]very catechist should be able to apply to himself the mysterious words of Jesus: 'My teaching is not mine, but his who sent me'" (CT 6, citing Jn 7:16; see also CCC 426–29). This is the vocation of the catechist. Even if we catechize only occasionally, so vital is the work of catechesis that the Church asks that it spring from a life freely "given up", a life of humble conviction, a life of glorious freedom through being rooted in the body of Christ and the obedience of faith.

An authority to define, for *holiness*

The *Catechism* teaches: "The Church's Magisterium exercises the authority it holds from Christ to the fullest extent when it defines dogmas"—in other words, the fullest exercise of authority occurs when it proclaims "truths contained in divine Revelation" or "truths having a necessary connection with these" (CCC 88). Pope Paul VI taught that "it is an outstanding manifestation of charity towards souls to omit nothing from the saving doctrine of Christ—always joined with tolerance and charity" (HV 29). We should note that Pope Paul speaks here of doctrine as "saving". The *Catechism*, too, speaks of dogmas as "lights along the path of faith" (CCC 89), and we know that the path of faith leads us to holiness, to salvation from all that is not holy. In fact, the Church's authoritative structure "is totally ordered to the holiness of Christ's members" (CCC 773). "All the activities of the Church are directed, as towards their end, to the sanctification of men in Christ and the glorification of God" (CCC 824; cf. SC 10).

There is a vital need to understand the difference between *doctrine* and *theology*. Doctrine, as we have seen, is salvific; it leads us toward holiness. The *Catechism* contains doctrine, not theology—theology being the activity of reflecting upon doctrine. It is important to distinguish, then, between the doctrine of the Faith and its theological explanation. And it is doctrine that is the province of catechesis. Catechists proclaim the Church's doctrine, her teaching; they do not teach theology. Theology is studied and taught by some; doctrine is to be known, received, understood, and handed on by all the members of Christ's body, without exception.

Some have asked whether the *Catechism* is a *theological* project, whether it has a "theological concept", which would be one among other concepts or other theological projects. Is it, they say, the concept of a certain school of theology? Of a Roman school, if such a school exists? Or of a "Ratzingerian" theology? Should it be discussed alongside other theological concepts—for example, a "Rahnerian" or a "Balthasarian"? Is this *Catechism* the product of a European concept of theology to be distinguished from an Asian, an African, or a Latin American concept?

The answer to these questions is that the *Catechism of the Catholic Church* is situated at a level that *precedes* theological concepts and that provides their foundation. The *Catechism* is not situated at the level of theologies, which are necessarily plural, but at the level of the rule of Faith (*regula fidei*), which is necessarily one, since the Faith itself is one.

In the work of the Editorial Committee of the *Catechism* there was, among the editorial criteria, one which claimed the first place: the matter of the *Catechism* is the teaching of the Church, the doctrine of the Faith. Everything that could be considered as belonging to a school of theology should be set aside from the *Catechism*. I will give you an example.

In the numerous reactions to the "Revised Project", which was submitted for consultation to the episcopacy of the Universal Church, there were many requests that the so-called "psychological doctrine" of St. Augustine on the mystery of the Blessed Trinity should be included in the *Catechism*, that is to say, the attribution of the faculties of the soul to the three Divine Persons: memory to God the Father, knowledge to the Son, and will to the Holy Spirit. Now you will find no trace of this in the *Catechism*. Why? Why this omission when the whole theology of the Latin Church throughout all the schools has more or less adopted this Augustinian doctrine? The answer is clear: because the Church has never considered this doctrine as forming part of the Deposit of Faith, or the rule of Faith, that is to say, the *ordinary teaching* of the Magisterium of the Church. No council, no pontifical teaching, has assumed that this doctrine formed part of the doctrine of the Faith. It remains a theological explanation, a very venerable one, but theological. The whole Christian East believes in the mystery of the Blessed Trinity without referring to this particular theological explanation.

The *Catechism* presupposes a clear distinction between the doctrine of the Faith and theological work. It is urgent to return to the distinction that St. Thomas makes so clearly in his famous Question 1 of the *Summa*. For St. Thomas it is clear that the articles of the Faith, summarized in the Credo, do not constitute theological conclusions but the actual principles upon which all theological reflection should be based. The articles of Faith have the same role as axioms in the natural sciences. They are presuppositions for all theological reflection. The latter does not formulate them but has as its task to explain them, to explain their implications, their mutual links, their meaning for human action, and so on. Theology does not judge these principles but works in the light of them. The role of magisterial authority, then, is to define *doctrine*, in this way providing the sure foundations for catechetical work, for the "good news", which is salvific and leads to the holiness of heaven.

An authority to define, for *unity*

God has revealed himself to us so that we may be one in him. The holy Deposit of Faith—all of the divinely revealed realities about who God is and what his plan is for us—is a unity. *Unity is the first principle of the Church's Faith*, and this fact necessarily governs the way in which the Faith must be transmitted. Catechesis is not so much an exercise in teaching topics, but rather an orderly and systematic initiation into the revelation that God has given of himself to humanity in Christ (see CT 22).

Our Faith is a unity because *God is One*, and the whole of creation depends on the One who gives it being. And this Faith is an *organic unity*, a living and complete unity, because when we proclaim the mysteries of Faith, it is not mere thoughts or ideas about God that we proclaim, but rather the living reality of God himself, whose self-revelation is personified and fulfilled in Christ Jesus. At the heart of catechesis we find a Person: Jesus of Nazareth, the Son of God (see CT 2). He is the living unity of God and man. Thus all words of the Faith always point to the whole: this organic, united reality.

Our Faith is an organic unity also because she through whom we receive faith, the *Church, is one*: she is Christ's living body and his Bride (see 1 Cor 12:12–26; Mk 2:19; Mt. 22:1–14), and our Mother and Teacher. We are reborn through the waters of *one baptism*, where the Church's one Faith is confessed and communicated (see Rom 6:4–5; CCC 190, 1253); and we are sustained day by day and week by week in the Holy Eucharist, where the faithful partake in *one Sacrifice*, and where the Faith is also proclaimed and lived by us in its highest degree because we feed upon the risen Body and Blood of our One Lord (see Jn 6:53; 1 Cor 10:16–17; CCC 1374, 1382–83). Indeed, the sacraments themselves spring from the Paschal mystery of Jesus Christ as "an organic whole in which each particular sacrament has its own vital place" (CCC 1211).

Finally, our Faith is an organic unity because we have been created for life in Christ: to live in communion with the Trinity forever, in the *common Spirit of love and unity*. Catechesis is not so much a matter of relaying information, as of being handed over into Christ, so as to be transformed in him. We have been created for that final immersion into eternity, when "God will be everything to everyone" (1 Cor 15:28). In that blessed moment we will see God as he is, face to face (see 1 Cor 13:12; 1 Jn 3:2; Rev 22:4). While we are on earth we cannot see the whole of the reality of truth, nor all its details, in one intuitive glance as we will do in heaven. However, we can still ensure that each individual truth, or doctrine, is seen in its fullness and richness by showing how it is connected to the whole of the Faith.

The overarching point is that, in God's great generosity, there is a continual unfolding of our Faith. Through the gift and work of the Holy Spirit, the Church grows in her understanding of divinely revealed realities. Our Faith today is the same as the Faith of the apostles. They transmitted to us this Deposit of Faith in which is contained, implicitly or explicitly, all that the Church has ever believed, believes, or will believe. Yet certain questions must first appear before some of these truths can be discerned, as for instance the first heresies concerning Jesus Christ. The Fathers of the first councils were able to clarify important questions regarding the divinity of Christ and the two natures in the one Person of Christ, and they did so in response to misunderstandings. Catechists today, as ever, must be vigilant in identifying and addressing commonly held errors.

How did the Church come to these truths? From where did she receive authority for judging what is true and what is false? Jesus promised his Spirit to the Church, the Spirit of truth, who guided the Apostles and now guides their successors to the whole truth (see Jn 14:15–20; Mt 28:18–20). Through the Holy Spirit, Christ has given the Church the wisdom to discern what is true and what does not belong to the Deposit of Faith. In this way, the Faith is constantly communicated from one generation to another through a living and active Tradition (see CT 22).

To conclude, the holy Faith of the Church must be protected and taught in its integrity and organic unity. We would have no access to the order of knowledge that is given in divine revelation, were it not for the fact that God humbled himself to become one of us and teach us the truth about his plan of drawing us into union with him. The source of the Church's authority to teach and the character of this authority flows from this revelation of the Lord and his gracious plan for our redemption. We may pray that each of us will welcome the authority of the Lord in our lives as he protects and leads us, through his Church, to the glory of his kingdom, in which we are called to abide in perfect beatitude.

—Christoph Cardinal Schönborn

Chapter One

The Craft of Catechesis

In this book we describe the work of catechesis as a "craft". The term is used here to evoke the notion of working with loving intelligence, uniting intellect, will, and practical skills in a patient work of drawing out the very best from the material with which one is involved. The ultimate Craftsman[1] in the work of catechesis is, of course, the Holy Spirit, the "interior Master of life according to Christ" (CCC 1697), and Mary is his "masterwork" (CCC 721). In her—and as her children—we, too can be crafted in the Lord (see Eph 2:9–10; CCC 1091).

This, then, is always the perspective for one learning the craft of catechesis: that it is a holistic understanding and application we are seeking, one that involves the heart, the mind, and the hand, and that we develop the skills of this craft as a participation in the work of grace in our lives; as St. Augustine said, "Indeed, we also work, but we are only collaborating with God who works."[2]

One of the central aspects of this craft lies in our coming to appreciate the significance of the Faith *as a whole* and learning to appropriate it and transmit it as such. The *Catechism of the Catholic Church* states that it offers itself as an organic account of a living *whole*, one in which the different elements are united and are presented in relational fashion (see CCC 11, 18). It asks to be read in this light.

---

[1] It is an image used by Plato for God in the *Timeaus*. Although Plato's understanding of the relationship between God and creation did not match the Christian revelation, the characteristics of Plato's Divine Craftsman, good and generously working with his material, and bringing beauty to birth, inspired much early Christian writing.

[2] *De gratia et libero arbitrio* 17; PL 44: 901.

This request for learning and teaching the Faith as a living whole is not something new.[3] Such a call is derived from the intrinsic nature of the Faith itself—as we have seen, it forms a unity, based on the unity of God and of his plan of salvation. The Catholic Faith is not a series of isolated propositions to be believed, but a unified whole, rooted in the unity of God. The believer makes an act of faith in God, seeing all things in relation to him, as St. Thomas argued.[4] The *Catechism of the Catholic Church* is calling for a holistic *understanding* of the Faith and a holistic *transmission* of the Faith.

The loss

The call is also rendered more urgent by the fact that an understanding of the Faith as a unity is particularly endangered today. In his work *After Virtue*,[5] the philosopher Alasdair MacIntyre proposes a scenario worth our consideration. He makes a "disquieting suggestion". Imagine, he suggests, that the natural sciences were to suffer the effects of a catastrophe so great that all that survives are fragments—parts of theories; half chapters torn from charred books; instruments whose use has been forgotten. Children would continue to learn by heart some surviving portions of the periodic table and recite some of the theorems of Euclid. People would discuss and argue over the fragments that remain. But the context of a living, knowing community of science that understands how the fragments relate would have been lost.

MacIntyre suggests that this illustrates the situation facing us today in the area of ethics, of morality:

> What we possess, if this view is true, are the fragments of a conceptual scheme, parts which now lack those contexts from which their significance derived. We possess indeed simulacra of morality, we continue to use many of the key expressions. But we have—very largely, if not entirely—lost our comprehension, both theoretical and practical, of morality.[6]

[3] The call is persistent. See, for example, Sacred Congregation for the Clergy, *General Catechetical Directory* (1971), 39; Paul VI, "Concluding Address to the Synod", Oct. 29, 1977; John Paul II, *Catechesi Tradendae* (1979), 21.

[4] *ST* I, 1, 3

[5] Alasdair MacIntyre, *After Virtue* (London: Duckworth, 1985), chap. 1.

[6] Ibid., p. 2.

MacIntyre then invites the reader to consider that words such as "virtue" and "conscience" have now been cast loose from the original contexts in which they were used, and from the living communities that could explain and illustrate their concrete, lived-out meaning. The sense of these terms is altered when their setting in use changes. We live, he suggests, in a devastated moral landscape and face the difficult task of careful reconstruction. Take "conscience", for example: when someone today says, "I must follow my conscience", this is generally understood as a claim reinforcing a subjectivist outlook; it means, in fact, "please don't interfere with my life; we all have the right to make our own lifestyle choices; you can't tell me what's right any more than I can tell you what's right." But this is not what St. Thomas Aquinas, for example, meant by conscience. It is not what the whole of the Church's Tradition has meant by it. But in much popular culture this *is* what is meant. "Conscience" has been removed from its setting within the Tradition, within the whole where it had a linked and integrated meaning. When catechists use the word today, those listening are likely to be "hearing" only a few aspects of the Church's teaching on conscience. Catechists may presume that others are "hearing" the teaching of the Church as she intends that teaching to be received and understood, but those being catechized may in fact only be catching fragments of that meaning.

MacIntyre supposes that most people remain unaware of this catastrophe in morality, and he argues that a historical investigation is needed to uncover the reality of the situation, in which one can discover such a loss. Drawing a careful comparison with the period when the Roman Empire declined into the Dark Ages, MacIntyre comments, "This time, however, the barbarians are not waiting beyond the frontiers; they have been governing us for quite some time, and it is our lack of consciousness of this which constitutes part of our predicament." [7]

That a comparable loss has occurred in catechetics is now well illustrated.[8] That there have been some recent gains as well is agreed, but the necessity of recovery, of *ressourcement*, was a preoccupation of the

[7] Ibid., p. 263.

[8] See, for example, Michael J. Wrenn, *Catechisms and Controversies: Religious Education in the Postconciliar Years* (San Francisco: Ignatius Press, 1991); Michael J. Wrenn and Kenneth D. Whitehead, *Flawed Expectations* (San Francisco: Ignatius Press, 1996), pp. 21–59.

Second Vatican Council;[9] and this is a theme consciously continued in the *Catechism of the Catholic Church*.[10] A "recovery" of the whole picture in the field of catechesis is needed.

Many adults in the Church today face similar difficulties to those identified by MacIntyre. Many are no longer aware of the Church's vocabulary of the Faith beyond a number of simple terms and phrases—nor is the meaning of these words and terms known, or how the various terms relate to each other. This is not a new insight, of course, nor a new problem. Jungmann's "kerygmatic catechesis", with its focus on presenting salvation history, ran into difficulties in the middle of the twentieth century because, despite its appeal, catechists did not feel the confidence to teach this sacred history.[11]

In his introduction to the *Catechism*, *Fidei Depositum*, John Paul II speaks of the balance between Tradition and *aggiornamento* (bringing up to date) in the *Catechism*:

> A catechism should faithfully and systematically present the teaching of Sacred Scripture, the living Tradition in the Church and the authentic Magisterium, as well as the spiritual heritage of the Fathers, Doctors, and saints of the Church, to allow for a better knowledge of the Christian mystery and for enlivening the faith of the People of God. It should take into account the doctrinal statements which down the centuries the Holy Spirit has intimated to his Church. It should also help illumine with the light of faith the new situations and problems which had not yet emerged in the past. (CCC, p. 4.)

But in many places in the catechetical world the desired balance has not been present: the huge emphasis placed on the quest for "relevance", on ensuring that all knowledge is "current" in a narrow sense,

---

[9] See Karol Wojtyla, *Sources of Renewal* (London: Collins, 1981); Alan Schreck, *Vatican II: The Crisis and the Promise* (Cincinnati: Servant Books, 2005).

[10] See Joseph Ratzinger and Christoph Schönborn, *Introduction to the Catechism of the Catholic Church* (San Francisco: Ignatius Press, 1994), pp. 11–15; Christoph Cardinal Schönborn, "A Time of Desert for Theology: *Ressourcement* versus Models of the Church", *Houston Catholic Worker*, vol. 19, no. 7, December 1999; Macellino D'Ambrosio, "*Ressourcement* theology, aggiornamento, and the hermeneutics of tradition", *Communio* 18, Winter 1991.

[11] Jungmann's most important work is probably his *The Good News and Its Proclamation* (New York: Sadlier, 1961). See also Jim Gallagher, *Soil for the Seed* (Great Wakering, Eng.: McCrimmons, 2001), p. 66.

has turned a process of updating into one of replacing. The resulting losses are keenly felt in catechesis.

It is important to understand what we mean by the "retrieval" of what has been lost in this context, and what is meant by *ressourcement*. It does not merely mean going back into the past to find something that has been mislaid or neglected. That notion would imply an understanding of Tradition as concerning only the past. The Church does, of course, look to the *past*, and hence to history, for her Founder was born in history and she herself has grown up through history. But Tradition is much more than this. The Church also looks *forward* to Christ, who is coming again, and she is aware of him as *present* to her as the Way on which she walks. She also looks continually *upward*, toward the Father, the eternal source and goal of all that is. Tradition is linked to each of these dimensions. The Church's Tradition is spoken of in the Second Vatican Council, using the image of flowing water (DV 9; see CCC 80), and this can be helpful to us when we seek to understand what is meant by "retrieval" or "restoration" in the Church. We are given the sense of a great river of Tradition, a wonderful, deep-flowing body of water from past to future and ever present with us. Pope John Paul II spoke of his desire that the *Catechism* inspire a renewal of catechesis "at the living sources of the Faith" (FD, p. 3), and this renewal can be thought of as a deeper welcoming of the river's flow so that the sources may truly penetrate deeply, cleansing our intellects and hearts. We might also note the *Catechism's* description of the Holy Spirit as "the Church's living memory" (CCC 1099; cf. Jn 14:26): here again we have the sense of the transcendent, yet ever-close Spirit, both guiding the Church into all truth and recalling all that is past.

Individuals and wholes

The loss in much catechetical work of an overall "framework", an overarching "picture" of the world, has been particularly destructive.[12] We have seen the way in which MacIntyre characterizes the

---

[12] See John Paul II's identification of the need for an overarching understanding of the whole of reality as a prerequisite for the transmission of the Word (FR 82).

understanding of morality today, as all too often simply a series of unconnected fragments. We can see the same symptoms in the field of catechetical materials. There is often a lack of any overall "picture" that would make sense for people of how terms, phrases, and individual truths fit into the whole.[13]

We may be inclined to think that this fitting of individual truths into a greater whole is an optional extra, not really important for assisting our understanding. Can we not understand something by concentrating upon it as it is in itself? Is this notion of an organic whole really necessary for our catechesis? Does it not belong to a level beyond that of catechesis?

The *Catechism*, in describing itself as an "organic synthesis" of doctrine, will not let us tread this path. Clearly, for the authors of the *Catechism*, the appreciation of the Faith as a whole, as a single organic body, belongs to the very essence of the Faith; it is not an adjunct.

We can see the necessity of an organic understanding of the Faith once we realize that our understanding of anything at all is dependent upon how it is connected to something else. For example, if we say "the sea is beautiful" or "the sea is calm", our understanding of this statement arises in part from appreciating how the terms "sea" and "beauty" or "sea" and "calmness" are related.

It is true that first of all we must know what the words "sea", "beauty", and "calm" mean in and of themselves. We must know their definitions. That is our starting point. The precise meaning of words and terms of the Faith must be a starting point, therefore, for catechesis. However apparently dry it may seem to clarify with precision the meaning of terms and concepts used in the Faith, without this initial step one cannot move forward in understanding. It is worthwhile considering what St. Basil the Great, writing in the fifth century, had to say on this subject:

> Those who are idle in the pursuit of righteousness count theological terminology as secondary, together with attempts to search out the hidden meaning in this phrase or that syllable, but those conscious of the

---

[13] A "picture" such as the great *exitus–reditus* theme of St. Thomas, which governs the structure of the *Summa Theologica*, seeing creation flowing from the hand of God (*exitus*) and the redemptive and sanctifying work of the Son and Spirit drawing all things back to the Father (*reditus*).

goal of our calling realize that we are to become like God, as far as this is possible for human nature. But we cannot become like God unless we have knowledge of him, and without lessons there will be no knowledge. Instruction begins with the proper use of speech, and syllables and words are the elements of speech. Therefore to scrutinize syllables is not a superfluous task.[14]

We begin with definitions, with the scrutiny of syllables. But then, having discovered, or confirmed, that "sea" means a certain sort of large body of water, and that "calm" means relaxed and at ease, we then have to place the two terms alongside each other. In the clause "the sea is calm", "is" does not signify equivalence but connectedness, and we need to understand the connection in order to understand what has been said. In any affirmation or negation two or more terms are placed together, and for an act of understanding to take place we need to understand the relationship of the two.

It is, above all, this connection of the truths of the Faith to each other, their interconnectedness, that has been missing from accounts of the Faith in many catechetical materials. And this has meant that those using these materials have been unable to understand the full meaning of the terms about which they are reading.

The *Catechism* gives us an organic presentation of the Faith. The annunciation of the Faith is made, not as a list of points, or isolated truths, but as a living, organic whole, in which the connections between the spiritual life and dogma, between the liturgy and the moral life, and between the personal and communal dimensions of the Faith, are stressed (see CCC 89–90). Time and again, the *Catechism* stresses that we need to think beyond individual dogmas or terms to a wider sense of the Faith and how these individual terms are located in this greater whole. For instance, when examining the question "Why does evil exist?" the *Catechism* states, "Only Christian faith as a whole constitutes the answer to this question", and it then goes on to list some of the elements of the Faith—"the goodness of creation, the drama of sin, and the patient love of God who comes to meet man by his covenants, the redemptive Incarnation of his Son, his gift of the Spirit ..." (CCC 309). Again, certain truths are said to shed particular light

[14] St. Basil the Great, *On the Holy Spirit* (New York: St. Vladimir's Seminary Press, 1980), section 1:2.

on other truths: "Only the light of divine Revelation clarifies the reality of sin" (CCC 387)—one truth is needed to illuminate another. This is said also of the commandments:

> The Decalogue forms a coherent whole. Each "word" refers to each of the others and to all of them; they reciprocally condition one another. The two tablets [tables] shed light on one another; they form an organic unity.[15]

In the same paragraph, the *Catechism* refers this point to the way in which we understand the Christian *life* as well: "To transgress one commandment is to infringe all the others" (CCC 2069; cf. Jas 2:10–11). The relatedness of the Faith applies to how we believe and also to how we worship and how we live.

The *Catechism* arrests the deterioration and disintegration of a coherent understanding of the Faith as a whole. The whole of Tradition is now presented for us, is summed up, in this definitive work; the rich vocabulary of the Faith is present; the fragments have been placed in their setting, not within some abstract theological "system", but as aspects of an organic, living whole. The *Catechism* has given us the opportunity to understand the wholeness of the Faith once more.

Alcuin of York and the craft of catechesis

We are in need of a program of recovery, and the *Catechism* sets us on this road. In periods of crisis the temptation is to take shortcuts, to look for immediate solutions that appear to resolve problems. In the field of catechesis this is the mistake of imagining that handing on and learning about the Faith is something akin to a technique that can be mastered rapidly. The *Catechism*, in its very richness, points us in a different direction, toward the realization that catechesis is a craft, and that catechists are being called to be apprenticed in the Lord's own school to learn the principles and how to work out this craft.

No historical analogy is exact, but an examination of how the Church has developed her educational work in other centuries can assist us in

---

[15] CCC 2069.

gaining insights into the steps we need to take in order to foster recovery in our own time. An extraordinary period in the Church's history from which we can learn is that of the beginning of the Carolingian period in Europe, with Charlemagne's vision of a renewal of the Roman Empire, but this time under the guidance and wisdom of the Church, a *Holy* Roman Empire. It was a time when the barbarians were indeed abroad, an age in which the flickering light of the gospel was kept burning by small dedicated communities, isolated monastic settlements, courageous bishops and their clergy. A deeper awareness of the initiatives taken here can also alert us to the parallels in what the *Catechism* is offering us today, for in fact the most significant initiatives were educational, pastoral, and liturgical. Charlemagne's preoccupation lay in *how to transmit the culture of the Faith.* It was to be a cultural renaissance, directed by the Church, which would be the chief means by which a Christian society would be developed. The glories of the past were to be revived; the liberal arts fostered; but the new Athens would have Jerusalem joined to it, the seven gifts of the Holy Spirit impregnating the seven liberal arts.[16] It was the work undertaken in this period that laid the foundations for the full flowering of the medieval synthesis between faith and culture.

We must not be deceived by many writers referring to the medieval, especially the early medieval, period as "Europe's cold Gothic tomb",[17] "the Dark Ages", or an equivalent phrase that would indicate something static, dark, dead, or even asphyxiating, out of which the Renaissance (rebirth) to new life took place, in the fourteenth century. What we term the "Middle Ages" was, in fact, contrary to much popular prejudice, a period of extraordinary activity, vitality, and creativity, whether one likes the Gothic style or not; in language, art, architecture, and philosophy it is unique and extraordinarily innovative—whereas the Renaissance was actually a return to the classic, static lines of a period that had died a long time before, a previous form of thought and a previous culture. Some historians, therefore, speak, more accurately, of a *twelfth-century* renaissance.

[16] The *trivium* consists of grammar, logic, rhetoric; and the *quadrivium* consists of geometry, arithmetic, astronomy, and music.

[17] B. P. Copenhaver, and C. B. Schmitt, quoting J. Burckhardt, in *Renaissance Philosophy* (Oxford: Oxford University Press, 1992), p. 19.

The key educationalist who laid the foundations for this renaissance was Alcuin of York, who lived in the eighth century (born ca. 732). He was a rare figure, able to unite an intense and patient concern for detail with a profound vision. As the chief architect of Charlemagne's educational reforms, Alcuin was long-sighted. He thought in centuries. He knew that his work was akin to that of planting oaks, raising a forest of faith that would be resilient, hardy, slow-growing but strong, able to withstand a hostile climate. Despite frequent setbacks, Alcuin's work survived and had enormous impact in time: "Like a fire in dry grass, it passed here and there, always alive at this monastic centre or that ... the fire of learning smoldered on under ashes".[18]

The successful seeding of faith in culture, he knew, needs to attend to the environment into which the Faith is sown, and this means especially the ecclesial culture. One needs a rich environment of liturgy and prayer; one needs the formation of schools of learning; one needs teachers; and one needs books. He knew that he also needed a common language, both spoken and written, for the cathedral and monastic schools that Charlemagne had called for throughout his empire. Alcuin therefore set about the introduction of a standard use of Latin in the schools that were being founded.[19]

Alcuin was no ivory-tower educationalist. He had brought from England the methods of making parchment, ink, pens, and brushes. One of his first requests to Charlemagne was to "stock the forests": no learning could take place without books, and so the most fundamental requirements were for enough deer, for making vellum, and wild boar, whose bristles were used for making brushes.

He also brought from England the techniques and standards necessary for the legible copying of manuscripts. Setting up schools for monks, he also introduced writing standards that are still our conventions today: it was Alcuin who decided on the system of spaces between words and paragraphs, capital letters at the beginning of sentences, and the miniscule script.

Once reading and writing had been learned books could begin to be copied. The books available to be copied at the time were few, and

[18] David Knowles, *The Evolution of Medieval Thought*, 2nd ed. (London: Longman, 1989), pp. 69, 71.

[19] See Henri Pirenne, *A History of Europe from the Invasions to the XVI Century* (New York: University Books, 1955), pp. 89–93.

they were often classical texts of Roman origin that were not Christian. All, however, were considered valuable for learning purposes—we have the beginnings of Christian humanism in this Carolingian period. Some books, such as the Bible, could take several years to copy, and a single monk could copy perhaps ten books in his normally short lifetime. It has been said that it took Europe approximately two hundred years to copy enough books for enough schools of learning for the development of a widespread high-level education, which was no longer confined to pockets of learning in the rural and often isolated monasteries of Europe.[20] In time, for example, the Benedictine monastery of Monte Cassino, high in the mountains in Italy, became one of the best defended monasteries and was able to maintain one of the three or four best-stocked libraries as well. St. Thomas Aquinas was sent there for his education and had access to an excellent library. One can draw a direct line from Alciun's stocking of the forests with deer and wild boar in the eighth century through to the possibility of St. Thomas writing his *Summa* in the thirteenth century!

Alcuin encouraged Charlemagne to distribute and make available his *Admonitio Generalis*, which included a standard curriculum for the two types of schools founded in accordance with Charlemagne's legislation, the cathedral and the monastic schools, ensuring that the fundamental doctrines of the Church were studied and known.[21] Key texts for study lay at the roots of the curriculum, which climaxed in the study of Scripture and the Latin Fathers.[22] "Alcuin's object was . . . to prepare young men in the liberal arts so that they could read and understand the Bible. The end, in other words, was spiritual, and the means were the liberal arts."[23] Crucial was the secure knowledge of doctrine, especially the doctrines of the Trinity and of Jesus Christ, the central planks of the Faith. Theological speculation could develop only on this stable foundation of knowledge of doctrine.

Alongside Scripture, Alcuin set about the reform of the liturgy. While not supplanting local liturgical traditions, and being always sensitive to

---

[20] See Knowles, *Evolution*, chap. 6.

[21] See Paul Johnson, *A History of Christianity* (Harmondsworth: Penguin Books, 1976), p. 160.

[22] Ibid., p. 69.

[23] J. M. Wallace-Hadrill, *The Frankish Church* (Oxford: Oxford University Press, 1983), pp. 196–97.

regional and local devotions, Alcuin gradually worked to lay the foundations for the Roman liturgy that we have today.[24] He encouraged a unification of rites, with a basis in Roman rite, but generously accommodating to devotional practices and liturgical styles in the local areas.

Let us draw together some of the insights we can gain from this period, and from the work of Alcuin in particular, the "greatest cultural transmitter" of his time.[25] They translate well into our current time and find numerous echoes in the *Catechism* and the contemporary concerns of the Magisterium, as expressed in writings on catechesis.

First we see the importance of the focus on formation, especially the formation of the person transmitting education. The transmission of the Faith is personal—through the bishop, through the master of the monastic school, or from master to pupil. It was an age in which catechetical resources were virtually nonexistent and certainly Alcuin was concerned with the development of texts for handing on the Faith; but these never replaced the person. We have a parallel in the declaration of the *General Directory for Catechesis* that the "absolute priority" is in the formation of catechists.[26] The role of the *Catechism* is as an "instrument" (CCC 12) of the catechist. There was never a question of trying to produce catechetical resources that would avoid the need for catechists to understand that which is being handed on; this would be to transform the catechists themselves into instruments. Alcuin helps us to appreciate that we must not conceive of catechetical formation and the production of resources in isolation from each other or set the formation of catechists and writing of resources in any kind of false opposition: sound formation needs to be supported by good resources. That said, however, the "absolute priority", as we have seen, lies in the formation of catechists.

Second, formation involves the head, the heart, and the hand.[27] Man is a unity, a creature who believes, worships, and acts, and what God has joined, man must not separate. The *Catechism* speaks of "the

---

[24] See ibid., pp. 212f; Gregory Dix, *The Shape of the Liturgy* (London: Dacre Press, 1945), pp. 578–84.

[25] See Johnson, *History of Christianity*, p. 160.

[26] See GDC 234.

[27] As Thomas Groome has observed in *Christian Religious Education* (New York: Harper and Row, 1980), chap. 4. See also GDC 238.

integrity of the person and the integrality of the gift" (CCC 2337),[28] and this can be applied to the catechist in the work of transmitting the Faith. It is, therefore, no act of the intellect isolated from the whole person, any more than it is simply an action of the heart, or mere praxis, that appropriates the heritage of the Faith and hands it on. The key lies in the formation of the whole person: liturgically, scripturally, in doctrine and through everyday life, and through the deepest work of the heart in prayer. As we shall see, the *Catechism* emphasizes just such a rounded formation through attention to each of the four pillars of the Faith.

In the third place, Alcuin brought with him a conviction that the context within which the transmission of the Faith flourished was that of friendship, *amicitia*.[29] Friendship between catechist and catechized is the context for the full reception of the Faith, and such a friendship is possible since it is rooted in Christ's friendship with each and the capacity of each for a self-giving love (see CCC 1468, 1617, 2347). Such a perspective enables a richly personal style of catechesis to emerge in which prayer and the virtues can take root. Alcuin sponsored what was later described by Newman as the importance of "personal influence", of heart speaking to heart.[30]

Fourth, we can see the attention given to the heritage of culture and faith, to a careful and energetic gathering together of these riches in an age where learning for a deeper humanism and to gain a wisdom beyond the immediate concerns of the moment were largely ignored or treated as unimportant. Alcuin's own library in York was set on fire by Vikings, but his painstaking planning enabled whole libraries of faith and culture to survive in a Europe foundering and struggling under feudal and dynastic rivalries, and invasions, or, in the words of the Italian historian Baronius, times of "iron, lead, and darkness". We see in Alcuin's patient, generous, and broad-sighted approach to the transmission of the Faith an inspiring example for our own

---

[28] This is said with reference to the virtue of chastity, but it can usefully be applied to the work of education, and indeed to any aspect of the Christian life.

[29] See Wallace-Hadrill, *Frankish Church*, pp. 197–98, 207. Some broader reflections of relevance can also be found in B. P. McGuire, *Friendship and Community: the Monastic Experience 350–1250* (Kalamazoo: Cistercian Publications, 1988).

[30] Newman's famous saying, which he adopted as his personal motto, is "*Cor ad cor loquitur*", "Heart speaks to heart."

time, when in so many cultures the work of catechesis entails possible martyrdom, a time "of the Spirit and of witness, but also a time marked by 'distress' and the trial of evil which does not spare the Church" (CCC 672; cf. Acts 1:8; 1 Cor 7:26; Eph 5:16; 1 Pet 4:17). Alcuin can also teach us that it is only on the basis of the retrieval of Tradition that creativity in theology and in application to culture can take place. This paradoxical truth is the central emphasis in John Paul II's introduction to the *Catechism*:[31] he stresses that the *Catechism* contains "both the new and the old" (p. 4) because "the faith is always the same yet the source of ever new light" (p. 1). "Guarding the Deposit of Faith", far from being an antiquarian activity, is the main impetus for mission: it is no accident that the call to *ressourcement* and to a new evangelization have occurred together in the Church.

Fifth, another feature of Alcuin's work that is essential for appreciating the appearance of the *Catechism* in our own time lies in the universal scope of his vision. Alcuin wanted to serve Charlemagne in his desire for an education that could reach to the far corners of the empire and that could serve all cultures. His insistence upon a standard language for learning, a common curriculum, and a recognizably common liturgy echoes the selections in the *Catechism* on a common Faith:

> Through the centuries, in so many languages, cultures, peoples, and nations, the Church has constantly confessed this one faith, received from the one Lord, transmitted by one Baptism, and grounded in the conviction that all people have only one God and Father [cf. Eph 4:4–6]. St. Irenaeus of Lyons, a witness of this faith, declared:
> "Indeed, the Church, though scattered throughout the whole world, even to the ends of the earth, having received the faith from the apostles and their disciples . . . guards [this preaching and faith] with care, as dwelling in but a single house, and similarly believes as if having but one soul and a single heart, and preaches, teaches, and hands on this faith with a unanimous voice, as if possessing only one mouth".[32]

Cardinal Schönborn, commenting on this passage, notes, "St. Irenaeus is thus convinced that the unique faith is not only a matter of heart and soul, but that she expresses herself also with a unanimous voice and therefore a common language. The diversity of cultures and

---

[31] See the introduction and two opening sections of *Fidei Depositum*.
[32] CCC 172–73, citing St. Irenaeus, *Adversus haereses* 1, 10, 1–2; PG 7/1: 549–52.

languages does not exclude the common expression of the faith."[33] It is a truth as radical today as it was on that first day of Pentecost. As St. Irenaeus insisted:

> For though languages differ throughout the world, the content of the Tradition is one and the same. The Churches established in Germany have no other faith or Tradition, nor do those of the Iberians, nor those of the Celts, nor those of the East, of Egypt, of Libya, nor those established at the center of the world.[34]

Finally, we should note the practical dimensions of Alcuin's genius. He is concerned with the conditions that enable the learning of the Faith, from brushes and books to the development of schools. As a true craftsman, he is also concerned with the specifics and technicalities that assist learning—paragraph and word identification, word spacing, and accurate punctuation. It is a concern that the *Catechism* shares: as we shall see, there is detailed consideration given to the design and format of the *Catechism* to enable an accurate and fruitful learning and teaching of the Faith.

Holistic formation through the *Catechism*

One of Alcuin's key concerns was for the holistic handing on of the Faith in all of its dimensions—liturgical, scriptural, doctrinal, through living in Christ and through prayer. This meant that in their own formation the educators and catechists of his time needed to receive this holistic formation themselves, for one can only hand on that which one has first received.[35]

Let us examine how the *Catechism*, in and through its very structure, calls for and enables a holistic formation in, and transmission of, the Faith. As we know, the *Catechism* is structured in four parts, relating to the areas of the Creed, the liturgy, life in Christ, and prayer.

---

[33] Christoph Cardinal Schönborn, "Address on 10th Anniversary of the publication of the Catechism", October 2002; translated by Dudley Plunkett from the original French. This appeared in *The Sower*, July 2003, pp. 5–9.

[34] St. Irenaeus, *Adversus haereses* 1, 10, 1–2; PG 7/1, 552–53. This passage is also cited in CCC 174.

[35] As St. Paul makes clear: "For I delivered to you as of first importance what I also received" (1 Cor 15:3). The principle is reflected in the medieval saying "*Nemo dat quod non habet*"; "No one can give what he does not have."

The *Catechism* is not arranged like this arbitrarily, but because these are the four dimensions of the Christian Faith, and therefore the four dimensions of a living faith in each one of us. The *Catechism* calls upon us to learn and to teach holistically—the *whole Faith* for the *whole person*. We can diagrammatically present the four-part structure as four points on a cross.

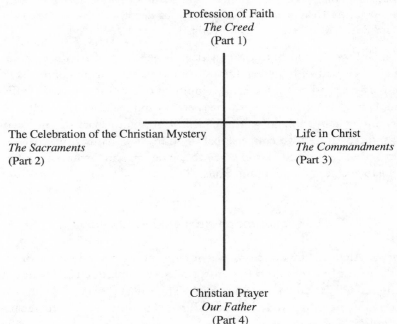

Profession of Faith
The Creed
(Part 1)

The Celebration of the Christian Mystery
The Sacraments
(Part 2)

Life in Christ
The Commandments
(Part 3)

Christian Prayer
Our Father
(Part 4)

That the Christian life can be conceived as having four dimensions is not an arbitrary decision on the part of the authors of the *Catechism*. One can find these dimensions in the description we have of the very earliest moments of the life of the Church. After the first speech of St. Peter in Jerusalem and the conversion of three thousand people to the Faith, we are given this insight into the life of the early Church: "And they held steadfastly to the apostles' teaching and fellowship, to the breaking of the bread and to the prayers." [36]

We are referred to this significant verse in each of the four parts of the *Catechism* (see CCC 84, 1329, 2178, 2624). The authors of the

[36] Acts 2:42.

Catechism are thereby taking us back, in the case of each of the parts, to the foundation of these dimensions in the reality of early Church life. The verse is also echoed in the prologue to the *Catechism*: "All Christ's faithful are called to hand [the Good News] on from generation to generation, by professing the faith, by living it in fraternal sharing, and by celebrating it in liturgy and prayer." [37] Catechetical formation, transmission centered on these four dimensions, was the pattern adopted by the Church thereafter, and it was enshrined in the *Catechism of the Council of Trent*, also known as the *Roman Catechism*. [38]

There are two images used in the *Catechism* to help us think about the functions and relationships of these four parts: *four pillars of a building* and *a symphony*.

Four pillars

The *Catechism* calls the four parts the four "pillars" of the Faith (CCC 13). The image helpfully reminds us of the necessity of each part: each pillar is important for holding up the roof; remove any one and the result is disaster. It is a vivid image with immediate and obvious catechetical implications. The image of pillars also helps us to think about the Faith as a dwelling place, a home, shelter, or perhaps place of worship. We build securely when the four pillars are in place in our own lives, and we foster a Catholic culture when we secure the Faith on the basis of these four pillars.

A symphony

Another image employed by the authors of the *Catechism* is that of a *symphony*, and this can be particularly helpful for our appreciation of the *Catechism* in a number of respects, including its basic structure. In the explanation of the logo on the front cover the authors tell us that in the pages we will find Christ the Good Shepherd, who will draw us "by

[37] CCC 3; cf. Acts 2:42.
[38] See Eugene Kevane, *Teaching the Catholic Faith Today* (New York: St. Paul Editions, 1982), pp. xxviii–xxx; Berard Marthalar, *The Catechism Yesterday and Today* (Collegeville: Liturgical Press, 1995), pp. 36–38. For an English translation of the *Roman Catechism* see that undertaken by Robert Bradley and Eugene Kevane (New York: St. Paul Editions, 1984).

the melodious symphony of the truth" (CCC p. ii). And in *Fidei Depositum* Pope John Paul II spoke of the "symphony of the faith".

Like most symphonies, the *Catechism* has four movements. Within these movements a symphony is made up of different notes and musical phrases, and this can be compared to the different beliefs the Church has about God and Jesus Christ, about the sacraments and prayer, and about how we can act in order to respect our own and others' dignity. Together these beliefs form one beautiful, harmonious whole. You may want to turn to the contents pages of the *Catechism* and just let your eye run down the different headings: these are the notes, phrases, and cadences of the living Faith.

We know that if we want to appreciate the genius of Beethoven in one of his symphonies we do not listen only to one of the movements, and certainly not just to a few bars of music from the symphony, nor do we ask to hear only the horn parts; we listen to all of the instruments playing together and to the symphony as a whole. In the same way, through the use of this image, we are being gently reminded to "listen" to the Faith as a whole. If we listen only to those movements or sections which have immediate appeal for us we will be unable to appreciate the genuine beauty and "genius" of the Faith. One can readily understand that listening only to the final, triumphant movement from Beethoven's fifth symphony without first hearing the opening of that symphony, which Beethoven described as "Fate knocking at the door", would affect the very way in which that final movement was heard, significantly limiting one's appreciation of the victory and cost of the victory that Beethoven was celebrating. In a similar way, to "listen" only to the fourth "movement" of the *Catechism*, on prayer, for example, would be to fail to understand the very roots of that prayer in the joyous life of the Holy Trinity and the Lord's gracious work of redemption. "This sequence is characteristic of the Church's prayer: founded on the apostolic faith; authenticated by charity; nourished in the Eucharist" (CCC 2624). The fourth part of the *Catechism* depends on the other three parts. No single pillar can support the roof alone. When we neglect aspects of the Faith, the very parts we retain lack the fullness, coherence, and attractiveness they should have.

The implications for our learning and teaching are clear enough. We need to be consciously aware that, since there are four dimensions of catechesis, so there are four elements on which we will want to reflect and four aims to be addressed through our catechesis.

Whichever "part" of the Faith we are mainly engaged in teaching, then, we are called to present it in a holistic way by ensuring that all of the key dimensions of the Faith are adequately represented. By doing so, we welcome a rounded formation in the Faith for ourselves and address the need for others to receive a similarly holistic formation. So, for example, if we are teaching about the sacrament of confirmation we will naturally be taking our starting point from the second part of the *Catechism*—the teaching is found in CCC 1285–1321. Our catechesis must reach out from this part and also relate what the Church teaches about the creedal basis of confirmation (part 1), the implications of the sacrament for our lives (part 3) and for our prayer (part 4). Every catechetical session, no matter what the subject with which we are mainly concerned, should draw together these four elements of the Creed, liturgy and sacraments, life in Christ, and prayer.

The primacy of grace

Before we leave our investigation into the significance of the structure of the *Catechism* we need to attend to one further point: the importance for the work of catechesis that comes from understanding the principle of the *primacy of grace*. This principle is reflected in both the weighting and the ordering of the parts. "The plan of the CCC is in itself a message", wrote Cardinal Schönborn.[39] A "clear catechetical option" was made by the authors of the *Catechism*—an option that they themselves discovered to be true also of the predecessor of the *Catechism of the Catholic Church*, the *Roman Catechism*: to insist upon the "primacy of grace", which Cardinal Schönborn explains as follows:

> [T]he primacy in catechesis is to be given to God and his works. Whatever man has to do will always be a response to God and to his works. . . . [T]here is a clear catechetical option, but this choice is not optional: it is self-evident. It simply corresponds to the reality: *God is first; grace is first.*[40]

[39] Ratzinger and Schönborn, *Introduction to the Catechism of the Catholic Church*, p. 46.
[40] Ibid., pp. 48–49.

The *Catechism* is first and foremost about God, not about man. The focus throughout is on the glory of the triune God and the mighty works of the Divine Persons in creation, redemption, and sanctification. It is true that man is searching for God, but much more important is the fact that God is searching for man. From the very first moment of our hiding ourselves after the Fall, God has been actively seeking and calling us (see CCC 410, 761).

Because of the importance of this truth of the primacy of grace, it is suggested that we think of the *Catechism* not only as made up of four parts but also as composed of two broad sections. If we think of it in this way, the *Catechism* can be compared to a diptych—on one side is a panel depicting the glory of God and his works; on the other side, a panel elaborating our response.

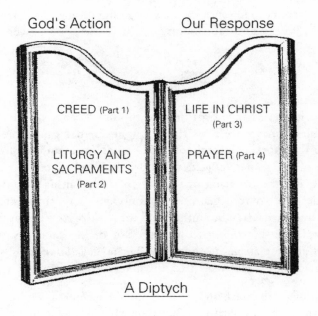

A Diptych

The story of God's action in seeking and saving his lost creation is told in the Creed—the first part of the *Catechism*. Here we have the story of God's gracing of his creation. The saving work of Christ is now available to us in the liturgy and sacraments—this is the subject of the second part of the *Catechism*. Cardinal Schönborn remarked that it is significant that these two parts precede those on morality and prayer, which identify the character of our *response* to God's saving work for us and in us. God's action comes first; how we live and pray comes second—though this, too, is by his grace. God speaks his Word into the world and it is through the hearing of this that we are able to stammer our reply.

The ordering of the four parts is vital. To have placed the morals part first might have suggested an altogether different emphasis, with the stress placed on ourselves and on our actions in the establishing of the kingdom of God. But this would have involved a misunderstanding of Catholic teaching, for parts three and four depict a response to God's calling carried out wholly in dependence on the work of grace.

Let us look at the morals part in this respect: we should immediately notice the title, "Life in Christ". The moral life, for a Christian, is not the fruit of human effort, striving after near-impossible ideals, of "dreaming the impossible dream"; it is the fruit of a new life, described in terms of both an incorporation into Christ at baptism (CCC 1694) and the reception of the Holy Spirit, who "having become their life, prompts them [Christians] to act" (CCC 1695). The Son and the Spirit are thus the two "hands" of the Father (see CCC 704), by whom we were made and in whom we are remade.

When we turn to part four of the *Catechism*, on prayer, we find again the perspective of the Christian life enabled and sustained at every moment by the grace of God. In the opening paragraph of this part on prayer we are reminded that prayer is a gift from God: "Man is a beggar before God" (CCC 2559).[41] When we raise our hands to him in prayer they are always empty, open to receive. This is why the definition of prayer given at the beginning of this part is so pertinent: "Prayer is the raising of one's mind and heart to God or the requesting of good things from God."[42] We pray as beggars, requesting the good things he so desires to give us.

And now here is the remarkable teaching of the Catholic Faith, so beautifully and powerfully expressed in the *Catechism*: what we would never have been able to discover, but needed to have revealed to us, is the condescension of God, who teaches us how to stand as beggars before him

---

[41] The *Catechism* here is quoting St. Augustine, *Sermo* 56, 6, 9; PL 38: 381.
[42] CCC 2559; citing St. John Damascene, *De fide orth.* 3, 24; PG 94: 1089C.

by himself coming as a beggar and asking us for a drink to quench his thirst (see CCC 2560). The passage in chapter four of the Gospel of John (Jesus speaking to the woman at the well) is used to explain how our asking of God and our desire for good things from him is only a pale reflection of his desire for us and for our good. God "thirsts that we may thirst for him".[43] The grace by which we learn how to pray, then, is a grace that teaches us how to pray from the position of being the beloved of God. In the *Catechism*, the New Testament is opened to us as a landscape of love in which we are privileged to see something of the incredible love flowing to us as we are incorporated into the Son and thus share in the love and joy shared between the Father and the Son. Another name for that Love is "the Spirit", and it is he who is placed in our hearts as a spring welling up to eternal life.

The weighting given to the parts is also significant: parts one and two account together for about two-thirds of the *Catechism*. This is another clear message to us, a reminder to us of where the emphasis should fall in our own catechesis. Catechesis is a joyful proclamation of the works and mercy of God, undertaken and expressed in our midst.

The catechetical implications of this principle are again clear, and we can begin to ask ourselves how far our own understanding of the Christian Faith and our catechesis reflect this principle, both in terms of the content of the Faith and the ways in which we order our catechetical sessions. We can ask ourselves whether there are ways in which the weighting, the contents, or the order, might be changed in order to reflect better the primacy of grace.[44]

---

[43] CCC 2560; cf. St. Augustine, De diversis quaestionibus octoginta tribus 64, 4; PL 40:56.

[44] The clarity achieved by means of this structure and emphasis should not blind us to another central principle, which flows from the truth of the primacy of grace and which is also vital for our catechesis: that of *our participation in the work of God*. It is important to mention, then, that the first part of the *Catechism* also includes an important section concerning man's *response* to God's revelation (see CCC 142–75).

In addition to the guiding principle of the primacy of grace, then, we are offered the principle of what the Jewish Catholic Karl Stern has called "the unutterable mystery of the 'and'" (in *The Flight from Woman* [New York: Farrar, Straus and Giroux, 1965], p. 273)— the Catholic Faith speaks of God *and* his creation, of God's plans *and* of man's free will, of man *and* woman, of Christ as truly God *and* truly man, of Christ *and* the Church, of our Lady as Virgin *and* Mother, and so on. The mystery of the "and" is particularly important when we come to consider the means by which the Faith is handed on, for it takes place

Twelve keys for renewal

Alcuin undertook to work, in obedience to Charlemagne, to bring about a long-term embedding of the Faith in culture. The *Catechism* today presents us with the opportunity to welcome a grace-filled restoration of Catholic culture through the craft of catechesis. Twelve-step programs are popular and effective antidotes for addictions, assisting one in facing and understanding the mutilations, false turnings, and falsifications that have characterized one's personal life. We can discover, by analogy, twelve keys for the renewal of catechesis in the light of the *Catechism of the Catholic Church*, which will enable us to turn from unhealthy trends and tendencies in catechesis and participate in that renewal at the living sources of the Faith that our Mother the Church desires for us. We have chosen the term "keys" rather than "steps" partly because what we will identify are not sequential points, although in terms of the ordering of this book there is a development and building that we hope will best enable a comprehension of each key and its acquisition. The points we identify are more akin to parts of a living whole, to use the image so clearly preferred by the authors of the *Catechism*. We call them "keys" here both because of their essential nature and to offer the image of an unlocking of great treasure, allowing the riches of the Church's Deposit to be more fully accessed. We can summarize our first two keys in the restoration of the craft of catechesis in this way: our catechesis is to be holistic and graceful.

KEY I HOLISTIC

We are attentive to the four dimensions of the Faith in our own formation and in our catechesis.

---

not only in a way that unites the personal and the propositional (which we consider in chap. 3) but, even more profoundly, in and through *a unity of God's action and man's response*. The Christian tradition of the East uses the concept of "synergy"—the joint energies of God and man—to describe this central reality of the Faith. For example, in the fourth part, the *Catechism* defines prayer as "the action of God and of man, springing forth from both the Holy Spirit and ourselves" (CCC 2564). Our Lady, of course, provides the model of that receptivity necessary for a truly Christian cooperation with the energies of the Holy Spirit.

KEY 2 GRACEFUL

In terms of the balance and relationship between the four dimensions of Christian faith and life, and their explication, we maintain the primacy of grace.

Chapter Two

An Organic Pedagogy:
Savoring the Nexus Mysteriorum

We have already considered the meaning and significance of the Faith as an organic unity, together with the need to recover a genuine understanding of the Faith through appreciating how concepts, and the realities to which they point, make sense within a coherent whole and a living Tradition. When we use the term "organic" we mean to indicate that the truths of the Faith together form a living unity. We might think of a tree: some branches are thicker and carry others, while the smaller branches with their leaves and fruit belong organically in and through these larger branches, thus contributing to the beauty of the whole tree.

We will now examine the *tools* given in the *Catechism* for *developing an organic presentation of the Faith*, in particular the use of the side references. The *Catechism* "aims at presenting an organic synthesis of the essential and fundamental contents of Catholic doctrine, as regards both faith and morals, in the light of the Second Vatican Council and the whole of the Church's Tradition."[1]

This chapter also paves the way for an understanding of catechesis as both "synthetic" and "organic", concerned with both "principles" and "life", with the Faith conceived as a living whole. Let us begin, though, by examining how the *Catechism* itself explains the vital importance of an "organic learning and teaching" of the Faith.

Visions of organic synthesis

When someone converts to the Catholic Faith he is not asked to believe in a multitude of separate things, each of which has to be taken and

[1] CCC 11.

25

assented to individually. It might look like this at first; it might appear as though one had to turn to the contents page, or the subject index, of the *Catechism*, and make an assent to each element of the Faith one by one. But this is not the case. When someone converts, he places his faith *in God and in all that God has revealed*. St. Thomas says that sacred doctrine is to be thought of as one thing since all doctrines are considered under "the formality of being divinely revealed". What is believed is "one and simple, yet extends to everything".

This understanding of the Faith is matched by insights that have sometimes been granted to the saints. For example, St. Ignatius of Loyola, the founder of the Jesuits, was allowed a vivid understanding of the way in which all of creation flows from the life of the Blessed Trinity.

> He sat facing the river, which at that spot runs deep. And while seated there, his understanding was enlightened. It was not a vision, but understanding and knowledge of many things.... All the helps God gave him during his whole life, together with everything he himself learned in his sixty-two years on earth, was less than the graces he received that day sitting by the river. Moreover, this enlightenment remained with him so that he seemed to himself afterwards a different man, possessed of a new intellect.[2]

In this powerful moment of insight, Ignatius said that he penetrated with his mind "all the mysteries of the Christian faith", seeing clearly how all created things were to be understood in relation to God— Creator, Redeemer, and Sanctifier—and how all of the truths of the Faith were interlinked in an unbreakable chain. Ignatius was granted, in a moment's insight, a penetration into the organic unity of all things in God, and in that moment his mind was remade in Christ.[3]

Alongside Ignatius' experience of enlightenment we might place that vision in verse: *The Divine Comedy*, by the greatest Christian poet of all time, Dante Alighieri (1265–1321). In this poem we have the theology of St. Thomas presented for us in dramatic verse. At the close of the third part of this poem, Dante offers for us a glimpse of paradise as a vision of God and of all creatures in him:

[2] Mary Purcell, *The First Jesuit, Ignatius of Loyola* (Dublin: M. H. Gill and Son, 1956), p. 91.
[3] See Rom 12:2.

In that abyss I saw how Love held bound
Into one volume all the leaves whose flight
Is scattered through the universe around;

How substance, accident, and mode unite
Fused, so to speak, together, in such wise
That this I tell of is one single light.[4]

The human capacity for God

An organic vision of the Faith is not only for saints and poets; it is for every person. The opening sections of the *Catechism* make this clear, in the paragraphs of chapter one, entitled "Man's Capacity for God" (CCC 27–43). These paragraphs provide us with our orientation toward an organic understanding. The sections are concerned with the desire for God (see CCC 27–30) and the knowledge of God (see CCC 31–35). The *Catechism* wants us to understand that if we appreciate the significance of our capacities for love and knowledge we will be able to see clearly why our learning and teaching of the Catholic Faith must be as an organic vision of the whole, in which each part has its place.

Love and desire

Let us begin with *human desire*. The opening subheading at the beginning of the first part of the *Catechism* is "The Desire for God". This is the *Catechism's* starting point for its annunciation of the Faith. We desire and love God because he is our ultimate good, our happiness. As Dante puts it, "Your soul is breathed in directly by the supreme Good, who so enamors it of himself that evermore it desires him." [5] This is the natural thirst and desire for God that is "written in the human heart" (CCC 27). We are created with an insatiable appetite for happiness. The *Catechism* refers us to St. Augustine's saying: "We all want to live happily; in the whole human race there is no one who does not assent to this proposition." [6] And so human love is a response

---

[4] *Paradiso*, XXXIII, 85–90.
[5] Ibid., VII, 142–44.
[6] *De moribus ecclesiae catholicae*, I, 3, 4; PL 32:1312, quoted in CCC 1718.

to what is perceived to bring happiness, to bring about our human good. Our love is directed toward particular things, events and persons who can contribute, or are thought to be able to contribute, to our happiness. We love strawberries, we love long summer days, and we love our friends. Our desire reaches out to all of these. As goodness "appears" to us in the world we desire it and seek it. But it is a divine longing that God has ultimately placed in us, a longing that leaves us with desire unslaked even after the many joys of loving and sharing in created goods. Ultimately, happiness is found "in God alone, the source of every good and of all love" (CCC 1723). Our acts of love connect us to particular creatures, but ultimately we will be satisfied only when we are connected to infinite Goodness, whose horizon of love embraces every created good. *Our desire reaches out to love the whole, and every part within that whole.*

Our desires point us, then, in the direction of the Whole within which alone they can be satisfied—God himself, and creation in relation to him. Desire and love point us to the discovery that all creatures find their place within a single, marvelous whole. Love is inseparable from unity. An organic approach to learning and teaching the Faith necessarily follows from the *Catechism*'s commitment to a pedagogy of love:

> The whole concern of doctrine and its teaching must be directed to the love that never ends. Whether something is proposed for belief, for hope or for action, the love of our Lord must always be made accessible, so that anyone can see that all the works of perfect Christian virtue spring from love and have no other objective than to arrive at love.[7]

We will have occasion to return to this paragraph again, especially in regard to its characterization of all doctrine as charity. Following the text of the *Catechism of the Council of Trent*, we can note immediately that *love is presented here as the source of doctrine and its end.* Love is the *beginning* since all doctrine has its source in God's self-revelation, and God is love. God reveals himself, and therefore it is love that he reveals. Love is the *end*, or *goal*, of doctrine since all that is taught is

---

[7] CCC 25, citing the *Roman Catechism*, Preface, p. 10; cf. 1 Cor 13:8.

for the sake of union with God in eternity, and since God is love, this means union with Love itself.

Love, then, is central to the pedagogy of the *Catechism*, and the *Catechism* is also helping us to see that unity is essential to love. As catechists we must ensure that our catechesis is inspired by love and directed toward love, and this means—even more fundamentally—that our catechesis must have its source and goal in unity, for unity is both the cause of love and its effect.[8]

It is easy enough to see how unity is the *effect* of love, since love always draws things together. But unity is also its *cause*, since one loves something because of an affinity that one has with it, or supposes that one has with it. Love always flows out of a subject's sense of co-naturality with an object.

Love flows out of unity, and perfect love must flow from perfect unity. God is perfect love and so he is also perfect unity: as we know from revelation, he is the perfect union of three Persons. This is God's "innermost secret".[9] This, then, is unity and love on the level of God, of uncreated being; and it is also reflected on the level of created being. Wherever in the universe there is individuality, unity, self-identity, there is also love. As every creature shares a likeness to God's unity, so it also, so to speak, loves itself.

We know, however, that a creature's unity is unlike God's in that it is not complete and whole in itself. It is also a part of a greater whole, and so must love this greater whole of which it is a part. Each creature is connected to this larger whole and oriented toward it. As Dante put it, "All beings cohere in an order, and this is the form by which the universe is like God."[10] The likeness of the universe to God lies in its order, in its organic unity.

We can already see from these opening paragraphs of the *Catechism*, how the authors are guiding us toward the realization that, as catechists, we need to work from a profound sense of unity with God, having a vivid sense of fostering amongst those whom we are catechizing the desire for God that is the deepest reality of every human heart.

[8] See St. Thomas Aquinas, ST I–II, 26, 27; and Étienne Gilson, *The Spirit of Medieval Philosophy* (Notre Dame: University of Notre Dame Press, 1990), chap. 14.
[9] CCC 221, cf. 1 Cor 2:7–16; Eph 3:9–12.
[10] *Paradiso* I, 103–5.

Knowledge and understanding

The second subheading in the *Catechism* is "Ways of Coming to Know God". Having begun with an examination of the human capacity to desire God, the *Catechism* now moves on to *the human capacity to know God*. We seek to know God because our minds are made for truth and God is the Truth. Our minds are made to know reality; this is the good of the intellect. At every moment the mind is seeking to know reality—we want to know the time; what is for dinner; how to bandage a child's injured finger; where we last left our reading glasses; whether it is true that our neighbor said such-and-such about us. We want to know; and this passion for knowledge, of our minds to grasp the truth of how things really are, reaches out ultimately to a vision of the whole of reality.[11] This might seem too grand a vision for our normally very limited reaching after knowledge; and it is true that we can rest apparently satisfied with too small a taste for knowledge—as for love—until the mind and heart are stirred to a deeper action and desire. But we can nonetheless appreciate the Church's teaching that this is the end for which the human mind has been made: the vision of an immense, unfathomable order of parts in a whole—not this time as the convergence of a multitude of loves upon infinite Goodness, but as a union with infinite Truth, with the divine Artist who knows every aspect of his handiwork. It is a vision possible to the mind of man because of the capacity with which the mind is endowed, "though not without great effort and only in a spirit of humility and respect before the Creator and his work".[12]

We have looked at the way in which the opening sections of the *Catechism*, concerned with human desire and love on the one hand, and on the capacity to know and understand on the other, both converge upon the same conclusion: that we find the fulfillment of these human capacities in an organic love and knowledge of the Whole. Moreover, in God we find not only the perfection but also the correspondence of knowledge and love, for in him we *know* all that we *love* and we *love* all that we *know*.[13] Above all else, it is this "loving knowledge" (CCC 429) that the *Catechism* wishes us to learn and to hand on.

[11] See *Paradiso* V, 7–9.
[12] CCC 299; cf. Ps 19:2–5; Job 42:3.
[13] On this, see Kenelm Foster, O.P., *The Mind in Love: Dante's Philosophy*, Aquinas Paper no. 25 (Oxford: Blackfriars, 1955).

The joy offered to the mind and the heart through the *Catechism* is that of beginning to glimpse the ordering of the parts to the Whole. When one teaches doctrine one is giving a taste to those one catechizes of the perfection of mind and heart that comes from the "vision" of God and of all of creation in him. This is the vision underlying the *Catechism*, and as a catechist one is feeding the heart's longing with ever-greater desire and exciting the intellect's energies by stirring mind and heart with glimpses of this ordering of creation, flowing from God and back to him.

The place of individual doctrines in the unity of the Faith

For the sake of an authentic catechesis, the *Catechism* is concerned to identify with precision the meaning of each individual doctrine and the distinctions between doctrines, so that each particular doctrine stands out, as it were, from the rest in its uniqueness. At the same time, the *Catechism* draws to our attention the relation and connection of each doctrine to the whole Faith. The authors of the *Catechism* are concerned with this simply because this is what it means to be faithful to the objective nature of reality, to the real distinctions and real connectedness of created reality.[14] "The order and harmony of the created world results from the diversity of beings and from the relationships which exist among them" (CCC 341).

Louis MacNeice, in his poem *Snow*, writes of the sheer wonder and dazzling nature of things in their variety, of a world of amazing singularity:

> The room was suddenly rich and the great bay-window was
> Spawning snow and pink roses against it
> Soundlessly collateral and incompatible:
> World is suddener than we fancy it.

---

[14] Compare the suggestion of the philosopher Robert Nozick (*Philosophical Explorations* [Oxford: Oxford University Press, 1981], pp. 415–22), who proposes that our scales of value may be linked to the extent to which we perceive variety and difference held together in unity, without compromising or diluting the difference—in other words, the idea of "organic unity".

World is crazier and more of it than we think,
Incorrigibly plural. I peel and portion
A tangerine and spit the pips and feel
The drunkenness of things being various.

Christianity shares this sense of wonder at the "suddenness" and
sheer variety of the world, and the wonder of each individual creature, whether snow, a tangerine, a pip, a rose, or a window pane. But
it holds that in the end the world is not "incorrigibly plural". The
universe is not a "multiverse"; it has a center, a unity; it is one (see
CCC 247); and it is bonded together without any sacrificing of real
distinctiveness of individual existents (see CCC 326).

The Church holds to this precisely because of her doctrine of the
Trinity. The Trinity is the source of both the particularity and the
connectedness, the unity of things. The Christian doctrine of God is
distinctive. It holds that God is both unity and Trinity. God is the
Father, the Son, and the Holy Spirit in a perfect communion of love,
of self-giving (see CCC 221).

The Father, the Son, and the Spirit are not three gods; neither are
they simply aspects, or modes, of a single underlying reality. They
are three Persons in one unity, distinct from one another in their
relations of origin (see CCC 254). The doctrine of the Trinity insists
on the oneness of God *and* on the full equality of the Divine Persons *and* also on their mutual distinction from one another. In the
Trinity there is at the same time the greatest possible distinction
between the Persons and yet the greatest possible unity. In its own
way, catechesis "mirrors" the Trinity in its attention to the individual doctrines of the Faith and at the same time their intrinsic connectedness in unity.

Learning and teaching organically

Having seen why an organic learning and teaching of the Faith lies at
the very heart of God himself, and also of ourselves and our capacities
(which we might expect since we are created in God's own image of
triune unity), let us now move on to consider *how* the *Catechism* enables
us, as catechists, to learn and teach the Faith in an organic way.

We must not think of this in any wooden way, as if there is simply a technique to be learned. It is more important firmly to grasp the principle of what we are seeking to achieve. Over and over again, the *Catechism* tries to introduce us into *the mystery* of the unity of the Faith, encouraging our contemplation of this truth so that it might gradually permeate our thinking and our catechesis. One important paragraph draws our attention to the way in which life, worship, and dogma cohere in the Christian life:

> There is an organic connection between our spiritual life and the dogmas. Dogmas are lights along the path of faith; they illuminate it and make it secure. Conversely, if our life is upright, our intellect and heart will be open to welcome the light shed by the dogmas of faith.[15]

The unity of these three dimensions—of belief, worship, and life—is expressed in the Latin saying *lex orandi, lex credendi, lex vivendi*—the "law", or rule, of prayer (*orandi*), of faith (*credendi*), and of life (*vivendi*) follow one another (see also CCC 1124).

A second key paragraph identifies "the mystery of Christ" as the point of coherence between the doctrines we profess: "The mutual connections between dogmas, and their coherence, can be found in the whole of the Revelation of the mystery of Christ."[16] This truth resounds throughout the *Catechism*, informing every aspect of its annunciation of the Faith. Thus, for example, in the case of the Scriptures, the *Catechism* teaches that they find their unity in Christ: running through all the words of Sacred Scripture "God speaks only one single Word, his one Utterance in whom he expresses himself completely" (CCC 102; cf. Heb 161–63); in the area of practical living, we are really speaking only of Jesus Christ, whom we must hope fulfills his promises in us so that we can live his way (see CCC 1698); and the Church, in the fullness of her head and members, is "*Christus totus*", the "whole Christ" (see CCC 795).

Ultimately one is dealing with a *mystery of unity* since it is derived from the mystery of the Being of God himself. We might take an analogy from numbers to assist us in understanding this. The human mind can comprehend and work with individual numbers—1; 6; 3,500;

---

[15] CCC 89; cf. Jn 8:31–32.
[16] CCC 90; cf. Vatican Council I: DS 3016; *nexus mysteriorum*; LG 25.

6,000,000; and so on. However large these numbers that we contemplate, though, we are still thinking on the level of individual, particular numbers and amounts. Now let the mind turn to the notion of an *infinity of numbers* and we are aware that we are trying to think something quite different. Within such a notion every individual number finds a place, no longer as one amount being added to another, but all held within a single concept. The concept of an infinity of numbers is a deeply mysterious one because it is not simply "the largest number one can think of", for one can always think of a larger; it is a concept of a different order altogether—and yet capable of containing all numbers of which we can think within it.

We find something analogous to this when we approach the truth that the Faith is one and organic. We are being asked to envision the whole of the Faith, all of the particular dogmas, within a single unity flowing from the triune unity of God. And, "concerning God"—who is uncreated Being—"we cannot grasp what he is, but only what he is not, and how other beings stand in relation to him." [17]

Having established these general principles concerning the need to bear in mind the uniting of the dimensions of the Christian Faith in our learning and our catechesis we might now say that, essentially, we need to learn to read the *Catechism* not only sequentially, but also across the four parts, the four pillars. Let us examine how one might undertake an "organic reading" with the help of the cross-references given beside each paragraph.

Identifying the topic

The first point is clearly to identify the topic that is one's focus. We have been looking, in this chapter, at the opening section of the *Catechism*, so we will take this as our example. As we have seen, the very first topic in the *Catechism* concerns the human person's desire for God, a desire that the *Catechism* says is "written in the human heart" (CCC 27). We turn to this section and find that it occurs in CCC 27–30. This, then, represents the initial scope of our learning and we read slowly through the paragraphs, identifying the key points. Our first reading is a sequential one. In chapter 6 we will discuss this basic

[17] CCC 43; St. Thomas Aquinas, SCG I, 30.

sequential reading in some detail. For now, however, let us move to the organic reading that we undertake once we have completed this.

Cross-referencing

Cross-referencing between paragraphs is one of the main ways the authors of the *Catechism* encourage us to help us make the links between the different dimensions of the Christian Faith in our lives and for the sake of our catechesis:

> Numerous cross-references in the margin of the text (italicized numbers referring to other paragraphs that deal with the same theme), as well as the analytical index at the end of the volume, allow the reader to view each theme in its relationship with the entirety of the faith.[18]

We follow the cross-references to the four parts of the *Catechism* in order to gain a clear understanding of the ways in which all four dimensions are connected to a particular topic. In this case we wish to understand how the desire for God is related also to the liturgy, to our life in Christ, and to our prayer.

We can see a number of cross-references, in small italics, beside the paragraphs we are reading, and so we begin to turn to them. Next to CCC 27 there are three cross-references, to CCC 355, CCC 1701,[19] and CCC 1718. These are our starting points.

- *The first cross-reference* takes us to CCC 355, which we notice is still within the first part of the *Catechism*, the creedal section. The purpose of this first reference is clear. In CCC 27 we have been offered an initial way of understanding why it is that the Church teaches: "The desire for God is written in the human heart": it is "because man is created by God and for God; and God never ceases to draw man to himself." We are enabled to see that God, as the source and goal of human life, draws man to himself through the engaging of our desire. God as origin and end of every human life is explained as the context for understanding this teaching of the Church

---

[18] CCC 18.

[19] In some printings of the 2nd ed. of the CCC, there is a misprint: 170 instead.

that every person has the desire for God as an indelible feature of his life. The first cross-reference, CCC 355, offers us a further and even deeper reason for the desire that has been planted in us—that we are made in the image of God. By leading us to this paragraph, the authors of the *Catechism* are reminding us to include this doctrinal point when we teach on the desire for God. Cross-references, then, offer us additional learning and teaching points and further reasons within the Faith for understanding better the topic with which we are concerned.

■ *The second cross-reference* takes us to the third part of the *Catechism*, "Life in Christ", to CCC 1701. By taking us to this part, the authors of the *Catechism* are reminding us to teach about the implications for our lives of being created with a deep desire for God in our hearts. CCC 1701 looks, at an initial glance, to be simply confirming the point we have already considered in CCC 355 about being made in the image of God. However, as we read the paragraph carefully we note that it is concerned with the identification of Christ as the image of God, explaining that we are each of us created and redeemed in Christ. We are made "in" the image of God, and that image is Christ. We are being asked to teach about the desire for God in our hearts in relation to our creation and redemption in Christ. Not only has God created us with a desire for him; he has redeemed that desire in and through the work of his Son, and that desire in us is now "restored to its original beauty and ennobled by the grace of God" (CCC 1701; cf. GS 22). The paragraph explains that Christ, because he is perfect man, "makes man fully manifest to himself". We are to look at the Person of Christ, and at the desire for his Father that governed his life, in order to understand the depth and beauty of the desire for God that is in our own hearts.

■ *The third cross-reference* also takes us to the third part of the *Catechism*, to CCC 1718, which refers us to the treatment of the Beatitudes: God has made us to find happiness with him and the character of that happiness is explained in the

Beatitudes.[20] The authors are offering us further scriptural references here for our teaching and also helping us to see that "the desire for God" has been spoken of as "the desire for happiness" in many ages and cultures. While not everyone recognizes that they have a desire for God (see CCC 29), all do recognize a desire for happiness, and the Church's teaching has always been to proclaim and explain that this happiness is ultimately to be found only in God.

So far, then, the cross-references have made links for us into two parts of the *Catechism*, deepening our understanding of the topic through connections to other aspects of faith and life. The other two parts of the *Catechism* are also drawn in by cross-references to this topic, and one can continue this organic reading in *two* ways.

1. *One can read the cross-references alongside the other paragraphs in the topic one is studying.* We can note that CCC 28 widens our view, by referring us in the text to the "prayers, sacrifices, rituals, meditations, and so forth" by which men through the ages have given expression to this yearning for God. We are being directed to the part of the *Catechism* dealing with prayer, to a paragraph that speaks of the universality of man's search for God in prayer (see CCC 2566). Another cross-reference stresses the moral implications of being called to offer worship, and we are directed to the first commandment (CCC 2095–2109).

2. *One can follow cross-references to the other parts of the* Catechism *from initial cross-references one has followed.* At this point we can marvel further at the rich connections and links the authors have encouraged us to find in the Church's teaching. For example, if we turn to the paragraphs on the first commandment we can see there, at CCC 2101, in a section dealing with making promises and vows, there is a further cross-reference, this time to the part of the *Catechism* concerned with liturgy and the sacraments, CCC 1237. This paragraph is stressing the importance of the promises that we make at baptism, when we confess the Faith of the Church. Again, if we move from CCC 1718 to a cross-reference indicated there, CCC 2541, we find ourselves offered

---

[20] In this section the *Catechism* is "retrieving" the work of St. Thomas in particular. See Servais Pinckaers, O.P., "The Desire for Happiness as a Way to God", in James McEvoy and Michael Dunne, eds., *Thomas Aquinas: Approaches to Truth* (Dublin: Four Courts Press, 2002), pp. 53–65.

the tenth commandment, which concerns being instructed in "the desires of the Holy Spirit who satisfies man's heart". From this paragraph we are referred on again to CCC 2764, this time to the Lord's Prayer, which can give "new form to our desires".

We will stop here—only because one must stop at some point—and sum up what we have found. We have seen how our learning about the desire for God has been linked to the dimensions of creed, liturgy, life, and prayer, enabling a full and holistic understanding of this topic. We have been led to see the underpinning of this topic in a renewed understanding of the person, made in the image of Christ and called to share in God's own eternal happiness; guided by the commandments to avoid the deformation of desire; formed and reformed by the habit of prayer; and strengthened by baptismal grace.

An organic reading is a deep and satisfying one. You might like to follow-up for yourself the remaining cross-references given in this short section, seeing how the topic being examined reaches out to all of the dimensions of the Christian life. It is important to realize, as well, that only a start in this process of cross-referencing has been made by the authors: each of us can be adding our own cross-references to assist us in our learning and teaching as we come to appreciate additional links and connections in what the Church calls the *nexus mysteriorum*—that is, how the different mysteries of the Christian Faith are implicated in each other. For example, next to CCC 27 you could add a cross-reference to CCC 2562–63, the passage that describes the meaning of the term "human heart".

When preparing to teach a particular topic one can plot the key paragraph references one wishes to use in teaching on a simple table.

Topic The Desire for God in the human heart	The Profession of Faith	The Celebration of the Christian Mystery	Life in Christ	Christian Prayer
27–30	355 368 398 843 845	1219 1237	1701 1718 2095–2109 2541	2562–63 2566 2764

Thus we can identify our third catechetical key:

KEY 3 ORGANIC

We practice an organic reading and teaching of the Faith, especially through the use of cross-references in the *Catechism*.

Chapter Three

A Personal Pedagogy:
Teaching the Living Realities of the Faith

In this chapter we will be seeing how the *Catechism* assists us in overcoming a serious difficulty that has made it hard to practice the craft of catechesis. Elements of the craft that ought to have been placed in a harmonious relationship have been isolated from one another. Catechesis has been greatly weakened in the Church for many decades over lingering difficulties concerning the relationship between *revelation as propositional* and *revelation as personal*. What do we mean by this? We can put it in the form of a question: As one is catechizing, is one acquainting a person with *knowledge of truths of the Faith*, or is one *introducing them to a Person*, the Person of Jesus Christ?

In the former category, that of the truths of the Faith, it seems necessary to place the whole of dogma, the whole of the "Deposit of Faith". Surely it is vital that a catechist hand on these faithfully to the next generation. And yet, it is often suggested, is it not so much more important to introduce people to the living Lord? In which case, is it not prayer, devotion, and spirituality that are of paramount importance? We can perhaps leave doctrine, dogma, and the study of the truths of the Faith to the more intellectually minded. Doctrine, then, is widely considered to be dry, abstract, and arid. It is said that doctrine, expressed in propositional form, cannot compete with the living knowledge of the Person of Christ. Catechists are to introduce others directly to Jesus Christ, not to knowledge *about* him.

Newman wrote about this common opposition that can be set up between propositional and personal belief:

People urge that salvation consists, not in believing the propositions that there is a God, that there is a Savior, that our Lord is God, that

41

there is a Trinity, but in believing in God, in a Savior, in a Sanctifier; and they object that such propositions are but a formal and human medium destroying all true reception of the Gospel, and making religion a matter of words or of logic, instead of its having its seat in the heart.[1]

This negative reaction to doctrine as an expression of revelation as propositional helps us to understand why it was so often the case that, even where the *Catechism* was not well received among those responsible for catechesis, the part on prayer was often singled out as "beautiful" or "helpful".

We can probably appreciate the point being made. We would think, for example, that something was wrong if we came across a married couple who had only met once, who lived in separate houses and who believed that marriage consisted in looking at photos and memorizing facts about each other. The Church's marriage to her Divine Spouse is about *communion* with her Lord and not simply gathering information about him.

Still, it is one thing to acknowledge that communion with another concerns *more* than knowledge of the other person; and quite another to deny knowledge a place at all. There remains an antipathy to doctrine in much catechesis that is worth exploring. We need to examine, then, the roots of this opposition that is often introduced between the personal and the propositional, and then look at the ways in which the *Catechism* responds to it. As we shall see, the *Catechism* opposes any sense that we are faced with a choice of either/or here; rather, the Faith is both personal *and* propositional.

Newman himself recognizes that it is possible that in some cases people may replace what he describes as "a vital religion" with "a dogmatic creed", resting "in the propositions themselves". But he emphasizes that this need not be so; indeed:

> Knowledge must ever precede the exercise of the affections. We feel gratitude and love, we feel indignation and dislike, when we have the information actually put before us which are to kindle those several emotions. We love our parents, as our parents, when we know them to be our parents; we must know concerning God, before we can feel

[1] John Henry Newman, *An Essay in Aid of a Grammar of Assent* (Oxford: Clarendon Press, 1985), p. 82.

love, fear, hope, or trust towards Him. Devotion must have its objects; those objects, as being supernatural, when not represented to our senses by material symbols, must be set before the mind in propositions.[2]

Rather than think of propositions as detaching us from God, we need to be aware of their absolute necessity in *attaching* us to God. Newman's own life bore witness to this:

> When I was fifteen (in the autumn of 1816), a great change of thought took place in me. I fell under the influences of a definite Creed, and received into my intellect impressions of dogma, which, through God's mercy, have never been effaced or obscured.[3]

Newman had discovered the converting[4] impact of doctrine, the "supernatural power of persuasion with which Christian dogma is endowed, when it is taught in its fullness".[5]

The *Catechism* makes it a priority from the outset to exclude any thought of a separation between a propositional and a personal understanding of revelation. The connection between the two is summed up succinctly:

> We do not believe in formulas, but in those realities they express, which faith allows us to touch. "The believer's act [of faith] does not terminate in the propositions, but in the realities [which they express]". All the same, we do approach these realities with the help of formulations of the faith which permit us to express the faith and to hand it on, to celebrate it in community, to assimilate and live on it more and more.[6]

Several scriptural quotations are carefully selected to open the whole of the *Catechism* and these precisely concern the relationship between knowledge *of* God and knowledge *about* him.

> "FATHER, ... this is eternal life, that they may know you, the only true God, and Jesus Christ whom you have sent" (Jn 17:3). "God our Savior desires all men to be saved and to come to the knowledge of the

---

[2] Ibid., p. 83.

[3] John Henry Newman, *Apologia pro vita sua*. (London: Dent, 1993), Chap. 1.

[4] It is described as Newman's "first conversion" by Charles Dessain in *John Henry Newman* (Oxford: Oxford University Press, 1980), p. 3.

[5] É. Gilson, introduction to J. H. Newman's *Grammar of Assent* (New York: Doubleday, 1955), p. 18.

[6] CCC 170, citing St. Thomas Aquinas, ST II–II, 1, 2, ad 2.

truth" (1 Tim 2:3–4). "There is no other name under heaven given among men by which we must be saved" (Acts 4:12)—than the name of JESUS (CCC, Prologue).

In the first quotation St. John writes of eternal life being a matter of "knowing" the Father and Jesus. This knowing is the fruit of a genuine commitment to him and love for him. It is a personal, intimate knowing of God. The second quotation concerns knowledge *of* God, knowledge *about* him. This is propositional knowledge.

By beginning with these quotations, the *Catechism* is reminding us that we need doctrine *and* we need personal commitment to the Lord. Our knowledge of God must be personal, springing from a deep inner commitment *to* him, and propositional, knowledge *about* God. The two are interdependent. Knowledge and commitment go together. As Newman said, we love and respect our parents when we know them to *be* our parents. We cannot love God if we know nothing about him. We cannot worship Christ without knowing something of his divinity. But on the other hand, we shall never know God fully *unless we love him*, and we shall never have a clear understanding of Christ's divinity unless we worship and adore him.

We can think of the apostles on the road to Emmaus (Lk 24:13–35). The two apostles were walking alongside Jesus, and yet they did not know him because they did not know enough *about* him. And so Jesus explained to them all the parts of Scripture that referred to him; he "opened . . . the Scriptures" to them. He told them who he was. And it was only then that they could experience him as their Lord and Savior.[7]

C. S. Lewis presented a useful analogy in *Mere Christianity* to help us think about the relationship between knowing God personally and knowing about God. He said that experiencing God might be compared to standing on a beach, sensing the power of the waves. Doctrines, on the other hand, are more like a map of the sea—far less interesting than the sea itself, but if we want to get anywhere and not merely stand on the beach all day we will need the map.[8] Doctrine is

---

[7] As we shall see in chapter 7, when we examine the character of catechesis as scriptural and liturgical, the disciples were able to recognize Jesus through his opening of the Scriptures and, inseparably, the salvific event of the "breaking of the bread".

[8] C.S. Lewis, *Mere Christianity* (London: Fount, 1977), pp. 132–33.

what we need if we want to be practical about the Christian life and start moving.

Doctrine is personal

The key point to bear in mind is that the Truth upon which doctrine focuses our attention is not an abstraction. It is not ultimately a set of propositions about reality, or a philosophical system. Jesus said, "I am the way, and the truth and the life" (Jn 14:6). *Jesus is the Truth.* When Pilate asked Jesus, "What is truth?" therefore, he was asking the wrong question, because ultimate Truth is not a "what". Truth is a "who".

We are called, then, to know the truths of the Faith, and to know them as truths belonging to the Truth, who is a Person. Knowledge of Jesus as the Truth sets us free (Jn 8:32), and *knowledge of doctrine as personal sets catechesis free.* All of our doctrinal propositions are attempts to formulate truths clearly. They are absolutely necessary, for they are not merely human attempts to know more precisely the Person of Christ and the Persons of the Trinity; they are Christ's revelation, allowing us to know his Father, his Spirit, and himself more precisely. Every doctrinal formulation is deeply personal. That is why there is nothing more satisfying, more exciting, and more enlivening than doctrines: doctrines are icons of Persons. "Creeds and dogmas", wrote Newman,

> live in the one idea they are designed to express, and which alone is substantive; and are necessary, because the human mind cannot reflect upon it except piecemeal, cannot use it in its oneness and entireness, or without resolving it into a series of aspects and relations.[9]

Creeds, dogmas, doctrines do indeed "live"—they are living truths since they are truths about Persons. In its essence, the Catholic Faith concerns persons, created and uncreated. It is because of this that the Deposit of Faith is something *living*. Consider the language used of the Deposit here:

> We guard with care the faith that we have received from the Church, for without ceasing, under the action of God's Spirit, this deposit of

[9] *University Sermons* XV, 20–23, cited in John Henry Newman, *Development of Doctrine* (London: Sheed and Ward, 1954), I, 2, 9.

great price, as if in an excellent vessel, is constantly being renewed and causes the very vessel that contains it to be renewed.[10]

In an address he gave on the occasion of the tenth anniversary of the publication of the *Catechism of the Catholic Church*, Cardinal Schönborn commented on this passage as follows:

> This is an impressive image that St. Irenaeus uses here: the faith, a precious deposit received from the Church and entrusted to us to be safeguarded with care, has the power to restore to life, and to ceaselessly renew its recipient, the vessel which contains it. I think that here we are touching upon an essential point for a clear understanding of the Catechism.[11]

The Deposit is living, and we describe Tradition as "living" because the Scriptures and the liturgy are alive with Christ, and with his Father and with the Spirit of life. In fact, creeds also, and acts of worship, moral actions and prayers, are *personal realities*; they are the activities and expressions of persons—of the Trinity, of angels, and of men and women. The realities of Tradition are inseparable from persons. Doctrine is personal.

Foundational personal realities

In an earlier chapter we spoke of the *Catechism* using the image of a symphony. We can usefully return to it now. As well as having four movements, which we compared to the four parts of the *Catechism*, every symphony has *main themes* that recur frequently. In an analogous way, this is also true of the *Catechism*. It is rooted in certain foundational truths that permeate every part. It is upon these truths that we need to base our catechesis. Some parts of the Faith are more important than other parts. For example, the *Catechism* has something to say about the immorality of reckless driving (see CCC 2290). But this is not as important as what it has to say about Jesus Christ. Using the

---

[10] St. Irenaeus, *Adversus haereses* 3, 24, 1; PG 7/1: 966. This is cited in CCC 175.

[11] Christoph Cardinal Schönborn, "Address on 10th Anniversary of the Publication of the Catechism", October 2002, trans. Dudley Plunkett from the original French in *The Sower*, July 2003, p. 8.

image of a symphony we can say that what the *Catechism* says about Jesus is one of the main "themes" that recurs in every movement, whereas the sentence on dangerous driving could be compared to a single bar of music.

One can identify the foundational personal realities at the heart of the Faith: the triune God, in himself and as he reveals himself in salvation history; the incarnate Christ, the Word of God come among us; Christ's saving work, the Paschal mystery, handed on now, through the Holy Spirit, in the liturgy and sacraments of the Church; and the created order of free persons. All of our catechesis ultimately concerns these personal realities. The text of the *Catechism* therefore rests upon, and makes available for our understanding, these personal realities, which underlie each of the articles and sections:

- God, a unity of three Persons, and his gracious plan of salvation

- The Person of Christ, true God and true man

- The Paschal mystery, the work of our redemption, handed on in the Church through the work of the Holy Spirit

- The human person, created and graced

We can show the importance of these themes diagrammatically, at the centre of each of the parts.

The four points of the cross find their meeting point at the center; and there are found the foundational themes, grounding every part. The *Catechism* has been carefully written and edited so that these four themes run like golden threads through all four parts and through every section of every part. One of the key elements in the craft of catechesis is to ensure that, whatever the subject you are teaching— angels, the sacrament of reconciliation, Jesus' teaching on the Jewish law, or whatever—you relate it to one or more of these key themes. Why?

First of all, because you will be leading others to appreciate the personal heart of the Faith, helping them to see that the truths of the Faith terminate in personal realities. Through doctrine they will be led to the living Lord.

Secondly, because in doing this you will be helping your students to see the coherence of the Faith, the way in which the "pieces" fit

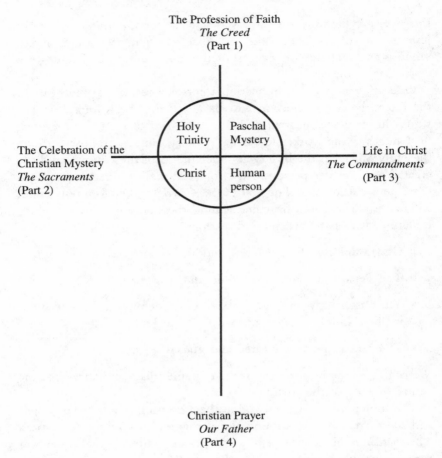

The Profession of Faith
The Creed
(Part 1)

Holy Trinity

Paschal Mystery

The Celebration of the
Christian Mystery
The Sacraments
(Part 2)

Christ

Human person

Life in Christ
The Commandments
(Part 3)

Christian Prayer
Our Father
(Part 4)

together. Thirdly, because you will be offering them reasons for the aspect of the Faith you are teaching: the Church's teaching becomes understandable to them, in that the items are seen to be drawn together in a beautiful harmony around personal truths.

The Church has a phrase to describe the way in which different doctrines depend upon those that are more foundational. She speaks of the "'hierarchy', or 'order', of truths". The Second Vatican Council said that doctrines "vary in their relationship to the foundation of Christian faith" (UR 11). We noted in an earlier chapter that we could describe some doctrines as being like the roots and trunk of a tree, while others are like the branches, leaves and fruit, which draw their nourishment from these great central doctrines.

For example, the doctrine of Christ's divinity is a "root" doctrine, while the doctrine of Mary as Mother of God is one of the fruits of this: since Christ is divine and Mary was his mother, Mary is the Mother of God. The authors of the *Catechism* thought it important for Catholics to be able to explain why they hold beliefs about Mary, the saints and so on. They can do this in part by showing how these beliefs follow from the foundational realities.

The principle of the hierarchy of truths does not mean that some truths are less true after all and so need not be believed! It would be a strange-looking tree that had roots and a trunk but no branches. It would be a sorry sight if the tree never blossomed into leaf and fruit. Moreover, the "leaves and fruit" beliefs safeguard the central beliefs as well as following from them. For example, the belief in the Virgin Birth protects the belief in the divinity of Christ, because it draws attention to the fact that God was Christ's only Father. As we have seen, Catholic beliefs are interconnected. We cannot take away any one of them without damaging another.

Let us look now at the foundational personal realities that lie at the heart of the *Catechism* and that we are invited to place at the center of our catechetical work.

1. *The Holy Trinity*

The foundational reality underlying everything is God himself, a triune unity. This is what the *Catechism* teaches about the Holy Trinity: "The mystery of the Most Holy Trinity is the central mystery of Christian faith and life. It is the mystery of God in himself. It is therefore the source of all the other mysteries of faith, the light that enlightens them." [12] The Trinity is the *central mystery* of faith and life: that is, of the Creed, the liturgy, and sacraments, life in Christ, and prayer. It is the source of *all* the other mysteries of the Faith.

As catechists, we often shy away from teaching about the Holy Trinity. We think this teaching too difficult for our students—and indeed

[12] CCC 234.

for ourselves—to grasp. This is why we can be particularly grateful that the *Catechism* shows us so simply and so clearly at every turn how to make links between each area of faith and life and this central living mystery of the Faith. Let us look at some examples, to appreciate how the *Catechism* helps us with this.

If we look at the first part of the *Catechism*, "The Profession of Faith", it is clear how the second section, expounding the content of the Creed, is trinitarian—because, of course, the Creed is divided into three broad sections. Thus we have chapter 1: "I Believe in God the Father"; chapter 2: "I Believe in Jesus Christ, the Only Son of God"; and chapter 3: "I Believe in the Holy Spirit". The three chapters have drawn our attention to the simple point that the Creed is trinitarian in structure.

If we then turn to one of the articles, we find the same trinitarian golden thread running through it. Let us look at article 9 of chapter 2: "I Believe in the Holy Catholic Church". This article begins by stressing that our teaching about the Church must be rooted in our teaching about Christ (CCC 748), about the Holy Spirit (CCC 749), and about the Holy Trinity (CCC 750). We are immediately reminded about the hierarchy of truths and about helping our students to see the connections between the Church and our doctrine of God.

After discussing biblical images of the Church, we move to a subsection titled "The Church's Origin, Foundation, and Mission". The *Catechism* then teaches, "We begin our investigation of the Church's mystery by meditating on her origin in the Holy Trinity's plan and her progressive realization in history" (CCC 758). The beginning point, then, is the Trinity. And we can now understand what the title signifies: the Church's *Origin* is in the Father; her *Foundation* lies with the Son; and her *Mission* is inspired by the Spirit. The paragraphs that follow expound this teaching, patiently demonstrating for us how the Church, at every stage of her history—from being a "plan born in the Father's heart" to the final perfection and gathering of the Church "in the Father's presence"—depends upon the work of the Holy Trinity, and especially upon one or other of the Persons of the Trinity.

The paragraphs that follow this treatment then look at the connection between the Persons of the Trinity and the Church again, this time not related to the historical development of the Church, but in terms of three key models of the Church: as the People of God, the body of Christ, and the temple of the Holy Spirit (see CCC 781–801). Thus we have a second treatment of the Church, once again trinitarian in character.

Let us turn to another part of the *Catechism*, part 2, "The Celebration of the Christian Mystery". Here we are beginning to look at liturgy, at the *Opus Dei*, the work of God (see CCC 1069). The opening paragraphs of this part straight away lead us into the heart of the mystery of the Blessed Trinity, with the first article in chapter 1 of section 1 being called "The Liturgy—Work of the Holy Trinity". Three sections trace the work of the Father (CCC 1077–83), the Son (CCC 1084–90) and the Holy Spirit (CCC 1091–1109) in the liturgy. We are being led to understand the ways in which liturgical and sacramental acts flow from the life of the Trinity.

What about the third part of the *Catechism*, "Life in Christ"? This again opens with a strong trinitarian dimension. The opening paragraphs refer us to the relationship of every Christian to the Father (CCC 1693), the Son (CCC 1694), and the Holy Spirit (CCC 1695). And, once again, the trinitarian theme runs through the individual sections of the third part of the *Catechism*, so that if one turns to the first article, on "Man: The Image of God", one moves immediately into the consideration that the human person is naturally created for communion with others precisely because he is made in the image of a *trinitarian* God, a communion of Divine Persons (see CCC 1702).

The fourth part of the *Catechism* is a profound articulation of the nature of Christian prayer. In the opening section, "What Is Prayer?", the *Catechism* describes prayer as "the habit of being in the presence of the thrice-holy God" (CCC 2565), and once again it gives us a historical perspective to enable us to appreciate how prayer involves our communion with each of the Divine Persons. Three articles treat of prayer in the Old Testament (CCC 2568–97), in the "fullness of time" (CCC 2598–2622) and in "the age of the Church" (CCC 2623–49). The age of the "fullness of time" is, of course, the age of the Son of God, while the "age of the Church" is the period of the Holy Spirit. Thus, once again, we are led into this part of the *Catechism* through the mystery of the Trinity.

2. Jesus Christ

The second "theme" (to use our symphonic image), or foundational reality, running through the *Catechism* is Christ himself. Jesus Christ, true God and true man, suffuses every page. The *Catechism* quotes from paragraph 5 of Pope John Paul II's encyclical on the teaching of the Faith, *Catechesi Tradendae*: "At the heart of catechesis we find, in essence, a Person, the Person of Jesus of Nazareth" (CCC 426). At the center of the *Catechism* we find, not a "doctrine", however profound and penetrating, but a living, beating heart—the Sacred Heart of the only Son of God (CCC 478).

The *Catechism* teaches, quoting from John Paul II again, that in catechesis "Christ, the Incarnate Word and Son of God, ... is taught—everything else is taught with reference to him" (CCC 427, citing CT 6). This is precisely what we find in the *Catechism* itself: everything is taught with reference to him. By taking this approach the authors of the *Catechism* help us to understand more clearly what doctrine really is; we are led to see that our doctrinal statements are simply attempts to know the Person of Christ more truthfully. Each is inseparably tied to Jesus Christ. We might say that dogmas are like refractions of the Light of the world himself, aspects of his infinitely rich life, introducing us to his Person and work in a thousand and one different ways. The dogmatic teaching of the Church on the sacraments, for example, has its foundations in the mysteries of Christ's life, since "what was visible in our Savior has passed over into his mysteries".[13]

Let us look briefly at some examples from the *Catechism* to illustrate this point. Notice, first of all, how often teaching on a particular theme opens with reference to Christ, immediately drawing our attention to the fact that all catechesis on the subject must be conducted in the light of his Person and teaching. For instance, we can look at the treatment of angels where, after preliminary definitions, we are told that "Christ is the center of the angelic world" (CCC 331). This point is immediately supported by three biblical references (Mt 25:31; Col 1:16; Heb 1:14) and the further clarification that he is this because angels *belong* to him. There are two dimensions to this belonging: first, they belong to him by virtue of the fact that they were *created*

---

[13] St. Leo the Great, *Sermo* 74, 2; PL 54:398.

through him and for him; secondly, they belong to him because they assist him in the work of *salvation*. Christ is the center of the angelic world, then, in terms of *creation* and *redemption*.

It is important to notice that the *Catechism* does much more than simply *assert* that an item should be taught by reference to Christ: it also gives us the *reasons* for this. The authors of the *Catechism* want us not only to know the Faith; they also want us to be able to "give an account of the hope" that is in us (1 Pet 3:15), to be able to offer reasons for the Faith we present.[14]

"Christ" is the word that opens the treatment of Tradition (CCC 75), the Church (CCC 748), and the teaching on man, the image of God (CCC 1701). And "Christ" is the word that concludes the treatment of the Eucharist (CCC 1405) and funerals (CCC 1690), and the culminating point of the section on the Amen (CCC 1065). These are more than mere literary devices. They reflect a constant concern in the pages of the *Catechism* that Christ and his teaching genuinely form the center of each article. What is said in the introduction to part 3 can be as truly said of every section of the *Catechism*: "The first and last point of reference of this catechesis will always be Jesus Christ himself. . ." (CCC 1698). Christ is the alpha and omega, the beginning and the end, the context and substance, of every article.

The authors of the *Catechism* explain why, in successive areas of the Faith, this is necessarily the case. Thus, for example, throughout the Scriptures God the Father speaks only one single Word, the Word who is his eternal Son (see CCC 102) and when we listen to the teaching of the Church we are hearing Christ's voice (CCC 87, 427); teaching on the sacraments must be centered on Christ because the Church's sacraments continue the works that Christ performed during his earthly life (CCC 1115); the moral life is rooted in Christ since he is the source and goal of our being (CCC 1701); and our Christian lives flow from our incorporation into him at baptism (CCC 1694). Finally, our prayer is nothing other than a glorious participation in the eternal language of love flowing between the Father and the Son (CCC 2564). A quotation from St. Paul's Letter to the Philippians very simply

---

[14] We will be considering this point in more detail in chapter 4, when we examine the way in which the *Catechism* assists us in understanding the Faith as eminently reasonable.

and beautifully sums up the centrality of Christ in the *Catechism's* presentation of the Faith: "For to me, to live is Christ" (Phil 1:21; cited in CCC 1698).

3. The Paschal mystery, handed on in the Church

The work of the Blessed Trinity in bringing about our salvation in the Paschal mystery is a further foundational theme in the *Catechism*. Christianity is a religion concerned with salvation, with the deepest issues of loss and gain, of tragedy and redemption. It is the dramatic story of the losing of all that is most precious, and of its restoration, long looked for and given beyond all expectation (see CCC 422). It is about man's capacity for an addiction to all that is base and squalid and his secret longing for the beauty of nobility. The *Catechism* teaches us that the Paschal mystery, that most momentous of all events in human history, of Christ "passing over" to his Father through his Passion, death, and Resurrection, sums up the whole of this longing and this suffering and enables its transformation (see CCC 2606).

As with the truths of the Trinity and Christ, that of the Paschal mystery underpins each part of the *Catechism*. Once again, let us look briefly at how this is the case. As we know, the first part of the *Catechism* is substantially concerned with the Creed, which is itself a summary of salvation history, of God's plan to save us. In much abbreviated form it tells of creation, the Fall, the Incarnation, and subsequent death and Resurrection of Christ. It concludes with the sending of the Spirit to continue and make present through Christ's body, the Church, the salvation won by Christ. The culminating point in this story of salvation is the Paschal mystery. This is the mysterious heart of God's plan, the cornerstone that is also the stumbling block (see CCC 1336). In the first part of the *Catechism* it is treated specifically in CCC 595–655 and the rest of the first part fans out from this section as spokes of a wheel around their center.

In the second part of the *Catechism* the whole of its treatment of liturgy and the sacraments is placed in the context of the Paschal mystery. We can see this from the main chapter headings in section 1: chapter 1 is called "The Paschal Mystery in the Age of the Church", while chapter 2 is "The Sacramental Celebration of the Paschal Mystery". The authors stress that the Paschal mystery is one of the key principles for appreciating the nature of the liturgy and the sacraments, those "masterpieces" of God crafted by the Holy Spirit (see CCC 1091). In CCC 1067 they make the point that the work of God in creation and redemption reaches its climax in "the Paschal mystery of his [Christ's] blessed Passion, Resurrection from the dead, and glorious Ascension", and they go on to say that it is precisely this "mystery of Christ that the Church proclaims and celebrates in her liturgy so that the faithful may live from it and bear witness to it in the world" (CCC 1068). In the liturgy and the sacraments, then, "Christ, our redeemer and high priest, continues the work of our redemption in, with, and through his Church" (CCC 1069). The treatment of each sacrament is carefully developed to ensure that this point is kept clearly in our view, with the personal heart of the liturgy and the sacraments thereby placed before us.

What about parts 3 and 4 of the *Catechism*? They, too, have the sign of the cross and Resurrection marked on every page. The authors have ensured that we have this perspective as soon as we begin reading part 3, "Life in Christ". It opens with the following paragraph, which is a quotation from St. Leo the Great, one of the most important occupants of the See of Peter in the early Church:

> "Christian, recognize your dignity and, now that you share in God's own nature, do not return to your former base condition by sinning. Remember who is your head and of whose body you are a member. Never forget that you have been rescued from the power of darkness and brought into the light of the Kingdom of God." [15]

The starting point for our catechesis about the moral life of the Christian is the reminder that it must be presented as a fitting response to the work of Christ, who has rescued us through the Paschal mystery. And a pithy phrase from St. Paul that we have already noted concludes the introductory section in part 3: "For to me, to live is Christ" (Phil 1:21; CCC 1698). For St. Paul, a description of the Christian life is as simple as that: to live is Christ. He can say this because he knows that the Christian life is always and only a participation in the life of the Lord, and especially a sharing in his death and Resurrection.

[15] CCC 1691, citing St. Leo the Great, *Sermo 21 in nat. Dom.*, 3; PL 54:192C.

The individual articles in part 3 proceed with constant reference to this point. It is worth noticing, for example, the way in which the teaching on man in the image of God stresses how the Passion is central to the restoration of God's image in us (see CCC 1708); how the Beatitudes are said to reveal to us the face of Christ revealed in his death and Resurrection (CCC 1717); how the article on freedom asks us to measure all understandings of freedom against that won for us by Christ on the Cross (CCC 1741); and how our feelings are "mobilized" to support us in our strivings to grow in Christian maturity precisely by our meditation upon Christ's Passion (CCC 1769).

The fourth part of the *Catechism*, on prayer, is similarly rooted in Christ's Paschal mystery. In common with each of the parts of the *Catechism*, the fourth part is in two sections. The first section of each part deals with general and methodological issues—in this case tackling fundamental questions such as "Why pray?" "Can prayer effect things?" "What are the main types of prayer?" and "What are the sources of prayer?"; while the second section of each part deals with the "details" and the "content" of the Faith—in this case by taking us through the petitions of the Our Father. The authors have chosen to make the Paschal mystery central to both sections by placing teaching on it as the pivotal point in this part—article 3: "The Prayer of the Hour of Jesus". This teaching concludes the first section and introduces the second. The prayer Jesus makes when his "hour had come" (Jn 13:1) is found in John 17. Called by Tradition "the priestly prayer" (see CCC 2747), it is the longest prayer in the New Testament, and the *Catechism* also calls it his "Paschal" prayer (CCC 2748): "It is the prayer of our high priest, inseparable from his sacrifice, from his passing over (Passover) to the Father to whom he is wholly 'consecrated'".[16]

The *Catechism* makes it clear that this prayer is not something that lies in the past, merely as an inspiration to us, or simply something of historical interest. Rather, it is a prayer that "extends until the end of time" (CCC 2749) and it is the prayer into which our own prayers are called to enter to find their perfect expression—everything, the *Catechism* teaches, is brought together in this prayer (see CCC 2748).

---

[16] CCC 2747; cf. Jn 17:11, 13, 19.

4. The dignity of the human person

Finally, let us consider the dignity of the human person, the fourth foundational theme underpinning the parts of the *Catechism*, the four dimensions of the Christian life. One might be inclined to think of this as a subsidiary, rather than a main theme. After all, the *Catechism* is profoundly God-centered, not man-centered, and it is the conviction of the authors of the *Catechism* that catechesis is to be characterized by teaching directly about God, and not merely about the human experience of God. But the Church has insisted that teaching about the dignity of the human person and his vocation to life in God is an essential part of the Deposit of Faith that is to be proclaimed (see, for example, GDC 123). This is the case because man is the only creature made "in the image of God", belonging to him, and like him, in a way that is shared by no other part of creation.

This is why the theme of man's vocation often opens a part of the *Catechism*; for example, part 1 begins with a chapter on "Man's Capacity for God", and part 3 begins with a chapter on "The Dignity of the Human Person". The doctrinal teaching on man's dignity is contained initially in two major places: first, the early paragraphs on the fundamental capacity of each person to love and know God because we are each made for him as our only and unimaginable fulfillment (see CCC 27–35); second, in the treatment on the Incarnation (especially CCC 456–83 and CCC 514–21). The *Catechism* asks us to remember that we are made *in* the image of God, but that Christ *is* the image of God; he is God. In other words, we are made "in Christ", and it is in him that we find our true face and dignity (see CCC 1701). The theme of the dignity of the person, then, is especially closely linked to that of Jesus Christ.

The *Catechism* helps us to realize this in a number of ways. One is by using phrases about our vocation and nature that echo those used of Christ. A striking example can be found in CCC 336. Speaking of angels, the *Catechism* teaches "From its beginning to death, human life is surrounded by their watchful care and intercession." [17] This picks up ideas and phrases from a few paragraphs earlier, especially CCC 333, when it speaks of the role of the angels in Christ's life, protecting him and serving

---

[17] In respect of this paragraph, the second edition of the *Catechism* (1997) altered the wording "From infancy" to read "From its beginning", reflecting the need for a complete absence of ambiguity in the face of a culture of death, which often denies the humanity of the unborn.

him from "the Incarnation to the Ascension". By echoing the words spoken about Christ, the authors are reinforcing the point that each human
life is surrounded by angelic care *precisely because we are created in Christ*.
This point is made over and again in different articles—for example, at
CCC 1010, on death, where we read, "Because of Christ, Christian death
has a positive meaning." What is true of human *life*, finding its true meaning and fulfillment in Christ, is also true of human *death*.

There is a constant pastoral concern in the *Catechism*, then, to show
how its teaching on God and on Christ has clear implications for our
understanding of ourselves. And this pastoral concern is rooted in the
dogmatic truths of the creation and Incarnation. It is most systematically explored in the section on the "mysteries" of Jesus' life—CCC
512–21, one of the most crucial sections in the whole of the *Catechism*. These paragraphs can profitably be read and dwelt upon many
times by all of us who want to teach the Catholic Faith—they explain
how we are united to Christ because of the Incarnation and how the
Incarnation is the basis both for our intrinsic dignity and for our day-
to-day living. Let us look at these paragraphs briefly.

The three paragraphs, CCC 516–18, open with a common formula—
"Christ's whole [earthly] life". The *Catechism* is teaching us that there
are three "mysteries", or invisible realities, being communicated throughout the whole of Christ's life: revelation of the Father, redemption,
and recapitulation. It is the third of these that is most important for us
at this point. "Recapitulation" is a word that means "sum up as the
head". Christ's human life is the *summary* of all God's dealings with
the human race, a summary that puts right what went wrong before,
and that stamps its own pattern on the rest of human history and life.

At the end of CCC 518 there is a quotation from St. Irenaeus,[18]
who makes the point that Christ experienced all the "stages" of human
life and because of this gave "communion with God to all men". "Stages
of life" is the phrase used to describe the fact that Christ shared and
lived through all the points of natural development common to all
people—he was a baby in the womb, an infant, a child, and so on.

If we now look at the conclusion to CCC 521 we will find there a
quotation from the writings of another saint, St. John Eudes.[19] It

---

[18] St. Irenaeus, *Adversus haereses* 3, 18, 7; PG 7/1:937; cf. 2, 22, 4.
[19] St. John Eudes, quoted in the *Liturgy of the Hours*, Week 33 Friday, Office of Readings.

beautifully mirrors the St. Irenaeus quotation: St. John Eudes says that it is *we* who "accomplish" the stages of *Jesus'* life and so come to share fully in the plan of God for us. Thus, Christ shared all the stages of our lives (St. Irenaeus), and now we accomplish in ourselves the stages of his life (St. John Eudes). Christ patterned his life on ours so that we might pattern our lives on his.

We have looked, then, in some detail at the ways in which the authors of the *Catechism* have embedded every article of the Faith, every doctrine, in the most fundamental personal realities that lie at the heart of the Faith: the Holy Trinity; the Person of Christ, true God and true man; the Paschal mystery, handed on through the Holy Spirit in the Church; and the dignity of man made in the image of God. These underpin every area of the *Catechism*. Ensuring that our annunciation of the Faith takes its life, its deepest meaning and its orientation from one or more of these will therefore enable our students to appreciate better the core mysteries of the Faith, their personal nature, and the coherence of all doctrines of the Faith in them.

Personal transmission of the Faith

We have seen that the pedagogy of God encompasses, in a profound unity, both the content of revelation and its manner of transmission. As we might expect, therefore, not only is the content of revelation personal; so also is its mode of transmission. And just as the personal truths lying at the heart of revelation may be captured in propositional statements, so these statements are also and necessarily attached to the personal acts that constitute the transmission of revelation. Of course, how could it be otherwise? To deny any propositional dimension to personal transmission would be to deny the natural way in which the human mind works, and also deny the human person a huge amount of his culture, in which the personal finds expression through liturgy, through the spoken and written language, through the handing on of the skills of craft and through the sharing of scientific knowledge. *In the areas of both the content of the Faith and its transmission, no opposition should be set up between the personal and the propositional.*

The *Catechism* speaks of "a specific divine pedagogy" in which "God communicates himself to man gradually" (CCC 53). And this communication, although it makes use of words, does not make Christianity a "religion of the book". Rather, "Christianity is the religion of the 'Word' of God, a word which is 'not a written and mute word, but the Word which is incarnate and living'" (CCC 108).[20] Christianity is better described as a "religion of the person". The *Catechism* uses an image from St. Irenaeus to explain God's pedagogy further: "The Word of God dwelt in man and became the Son of man in order to accustom man to perceive God and to accustom God to dwell in man, according to the Father's pleasure."[21]

In two places, the *Catechism* illustrates God's personal pedagogy, his gradual communication with man, accustoming man to his voice. CCC 54–67 identifies the "stages" of this revelation, developed in the form of covenants with those he chose—Noah, Abraham, Moses—and then his gradual formation of his people through the voices of his prophets. CCC 2566–89 reflects on the human response to this revelation and how it was articulated through the prayer of Abraham, Moses, David, and Elijah and in the assembly of the people of Israel. In all cases we see that the pedagogy is one of *personal transmission*, in which God seeks man out and elicits a response (CCC 2567). God reveals his Word and his Spirit to particular individuals and to a particular people, and it is for them to carry this Word and Spirit to others.

God's pedagogy culminates in the personal word of an angel speaking to the Daughter of Zion, the "purest figure" among those holy women who had kept alive the hope of salvation (CCC 64). "Mary was invited to conceive him in whom the 'whole fullness of deity' would dwell 'bodily'" (CCC 484, citing Col 2:9). The fullness of revelation, of God himself, takes flesh in the womb of Mary, and it is this enfleshed Word, through the power of the Holy Spirit, that is then carried to Elizabeth, so that her own child leaps in the womb in recognition (Lk 1:44). God's pedagogy is for the sake of his becoming flesh, so that, in him, our flesh might partake of his own nature and life. "O marvelous exchange! Man's Creator has become man, born of the Virgin. We have been made sharers in the divinity of Christ who humbled himself to share in our humanity."[22]

---

[20] The *Catechism* here is citing St. Bernard, *S.missus est hom.* 4, 11; PL 183:86.

[21] St. Irenaeus, *Adversus haereses* 3, 20, 2; PG 7/1: 944; cf. 3, 17, 1; 4, 12, 4; 4, 21, 3. This is cited in CCC 53.

[22] CCC 526, citing LH, Antiphon 1 of Evening Prayer for Jan. 1.

The embodied transmission of revelation, handed on in the beauty of the Word Made Flesh, is the central theme of the New Testament.

> That which was from the beginning, which we have heard, which we have seen with our eyes, which we have looked upon and touched with our hands, concerning the word of life—the life was made manifest, and we saw it, and testify to it, and proclaim to you the eternal life which was with the Father and was made manifest to us—that which we have seen and heard we proclaim also to you, so that you may have fellowship with us; and our fellowship is with the Father and with his Son Jesus Christ.[23]

The apostles proclaim the Word of life, which they have touched, seen and heard. In his classic work *The Meaning of Tradition*, Yves Congar cites Charles Péguy, who offers a poetically expressed statement of the Christian understanding of the ongoing transmission of revelation in the life of the Church:

> Just as at the church door, on Sundays and feastdays,
> When we go to Mass,
> Or at funerals,
> We pass holy water to each other from hand to hand,
> One to another, one after the other,
> Directly from hand to hand, or pass a piece of blessed
>   bread dipped in holy water,
> To make the sign of the cross, upon ourselves, the living,
>   or on the coffins of the dead,
> So that step by step the same sign of the cross is, as it
>   were, carried by the same water....
> In the same way, from hand to hand, from fingers to fingers,
> From finger-tip to finger-tip, the everlasting generations
> Who go to Mass age after age,
> One generation succeeding another,
> Pass on the word of God, in the same hope,
> In the same breasts, in the same hearts, until the world
>   itself is buried.[24]

---

[23] I Jn 1:1–3.

[24] From Péguy, *The Portal of the Mystery of Hope*, quoted in Yves Congar, *The Meaning of Tradition* (San Francisco: Ignatius Press, 2004), p 11.

The Faith is handed on from person to person, from fingertip to fingertip. An understanding of the etymology of "catechesis" assists us in the appreciation of this; it is derived from the Greek word "cate-chein", originally meaning "to echo".[25] In the time of St. Paul it was used to mean "to hear", "to learn", or "to instruct". Catechesis, then, is the "echoing" or "resounding" of a message. It is handing on what has been received. That is what St. Paul meant when he said that "I delivered to you ... what I also received" (1 Cor 15:3). St. Paul has received the message, and now he is "echoing" it on to others. To be a catechist is to receive, and to hand on what has been received.

We have seen the pivotal role that the apostles had in the initial transmission of the living Word; having been touched and seen by Christ, their memories and their Faith now stand at the root of the Scriptures and at the heart of Tradition, through which the Faith continues to be handed on to each generation. They themselves handed on to others (whom the New Testament calls "overseers", "bishops") the responsibility for maintaining "oversight", under the guidance of the Holy Spirit, of this personal transmission of the Faith. The Church teaches that these stand *"in persona Christi Capitis"*—in the place of the person of Christ the Head (see CCC 1548). Because of the essentially personal nature of the transmission of Christ and his message, St. Irenaeus insisted that, in order to be part of the community of Faith, one needed to be in communion with this particular line of succession from the apostles.[26] Personal attachment to Christ is made available through the priest, who "continues the work of redemption on earth".[27]

It is important to realize that when the Church speaks of the personal she does not oppose this to the social; rather, the person is intrinsically social: "Society is not for him an extraneous addition but a requirement of his nature" (CCC 1879). Therefore, "a *society* is a group of persons bound together organically by a principle of unity that goes beyond each one of them" (CCC 1880). When we are thinking of the transmission of the Faith, then, *personal transmission implies ecclesial*

[25] See Colin Brown, ed., *The New International Dictionary of New Testament Theology* (Milton Keynes: Paternoster Press, 1978), 3:771–72.

[26] St. Irenaeus, *Adversus haereses*, 5, 20, 1: PG 7/1:1177.

[27] CCC 1589, citing the Curé of Ars, St. John Vianney, quoted in B. Nodet, *Jean-Marie Vianney: Curé d'Ars* (Le Puy, 1958), p. 100.

transmission. The Word of God lives in *the Church* and through the apostles and their successors, through the sacraments, liturgy, and life of the Church, and through the Holy Scriptures, the Holy Spirit hands on that Word, from generation to generation.

In order to foster the integration of the doctrinal and the personal in our teaching and in our appreciation of the personal nature of the transmission of the Faith, we can use the following questions as a basis for evaluating our resources and planning our catechetical sessions:

- Is the whole clearly rooted in the life and work of the Holy Trinity?

- Is it clear how the topic flows out of the life and work of Jesus Christ?

- Does the treatment of the topic highlight the Paschal mystery, handed on by the Holy Spirit in the Church?

- Is it clear how the topic enhances our understanding of who we are and our vocation to life in grace and the Trinity?

- Is it clear how the doctrines being presented lead those whom we are teaching to discover and know the Lord more deeply?

So we come to the fourth catechetical key:

KEY 4 PERSONAL

We are aware that doctrine and its transmission is essentially personal, and we ground catechesis in the living foundational realities of the Faith, handing ourselves over to serve the transmission of Christ and his message.

Chapter Four

A Realist Pedagogy: Teaching the Faith as One, True, Good, and Beautiful

Oneness

The *Catechism*, as we have seen, emphasizes the oneness of the Faith, its organic nature. "One-ness", or "unity", is one of the "transcendental properties of Being". What is meant by this phrase is that unity is true not only of particular beings, but of all beings. The characteristic of unity transcends, as it were, the singular, and is true universally. Everything that exists has a unity of its own, appropriate to its own nature. Moreover, the "transcendentals" are not only properties of created beings, but of Uncreated Being as well—that is, of God himself.

The *Catechism of the Catholic Church* also alerts us to the importance of the other transcendentals within God's pedagogy: it offers us an understanding of the Faith not only as one, but also as *true, good,* and *beautiful*. The Catechism presents the Faith in this way, quite simply, because it is a proclamation of God's revelation. And what God reveals is himself and his plan for creation. God himself *is* one, true, good, and beautiful in his uncreated and infinite Being. And the whole of creation reflects this: each creature is beautiful in its own way, each has truth and goodness in its own way, each thing holds together with a unity of its own. These transcendental properties of Being are shared by every single thing that is, whatever the differences between them.

In this chapter we examine the importance of each of these for the pedagogy of God. We will look at the *Catechism*'s exposition in relation to each of the transcendentals and explore practical implications for this our catechesis. For example, the *Catechism* helps us to see how common misunderstandings of the Faith can be avoided once attention is

given to the unity of the Faith. This is because many errors in catechetics follow from a "mutilation" of the Church's teaching arising from
a lack of understanding of the bonds between doctrines. Again, the mistake of separating, or even opposing, pastoral and doctrinal discussions
of questions arises through an insufficient appreciation of the Faith as
good.

The image on the cover of the *Catechism* was selected to portray
some of the main themes and concerns of the *Catechism*. An examination of this logo reveals that it also illustrates the transcendentals.
We have seen that the authors of the *Catechism* provide an explanation
of the meaning of the image on the cover. We can read it again: "Christ,
the Good Shepherd who leads and protects his faithful (the lamb) by
his authority (the staff), draws them by the melodious symphony of
the truth (the panpipes), and makes them lie down in the shade of the
tree of life. . . ." (CCC, p. ii.)

We might pay attention in particular to the phrase describing the
panpipes, "draws them by the melodious symphony of the truth". This
is the *Catechism*'s own testimony to the attractive power of doctrine. A
careful reading of this phrase also reveals that the *Catechism* is uniting
here the different transcendentals. "Draws" indicates the *goodness* of
doctrine: the Tradition of the Church often speaks of God "drawing"
us to himself as our supreme good; we are attracted to God because
he is our fulfillment. Where the *Catechism* writes of the human desire
for happiness, it notes that God harnesses this desire in order to "draw"
us to himself as the supreme goal that we seek (see CCC 1718). The
phrase also uses the image of the "melodious symphony", an aesthetic
image, an image of *beauty*. And then it speaks also of "the *truth*".
Beauty is being seen here as a sort of bait to draw one toward goodness and truth. The *Catechism* conceives of itself as a melody holding
the faithful lamb attentive to the shepherd. It is important to appreciate that the Church always holds the transcendentals together; they
are inseparable. Beauty isolated from truth is merely hollow; the melody, deceptive; the player, a Pied Piper luring rats on to their destruction. Beauty isolated from goodness would be a shallow aestheticism.
Genuine beauty is always accompanied by the other transcendentals:
truth, goodness, and unity. The explanation of the logo, then, gathers
beauty, goodness, and truth into unity and raises our expectation that
this is how the *Catechism* will be presenting the Faith within its pages.

Truth

We have looked in an earlier chapter at the oneness of the Faith. We can turn now, then, to consider the Faith as *true*. We need first of all to understand the relationship between what is *true* and what is *real*. What is true depends entirely upon what is real. *So to claim that the Faith is true is to assert in the first place that it is real.* When we catechize, we are not proclaiming our own wishful thinking; nor are we speaking about some ideal but ultimately unreal world. Neither are we giving merely our own "opinions" on matters religious; rather, at every point we are speaking about what is ultimately *real*.

Then, in the second place, to say that the Faith is true means that *it is knowable by the mind*. When the Church teaches that an element of the Faith is "true" she means to say, not only that it is real, but also that this element is attainable by the human person, that we can truly know it. This will not be a full and complete knowledge, for what is real is always greater and more wonderful than our knowledge of it. But we can have a genuine knowledge of it nonetheless. This is why we are asked to give an *assent of faith* to what is proposed for us to believe. The assent we give is our affirmation that we *truly* know what is proposed to us without ever knowing it *fully*.

What this understanding of the Faith as true leads us to, then, is both *the real as knowable* and *the real as a mystery of Being* always greater than our knowledge of it. The *Catechism* emphasizes the importance of both of these for our catechesis. The opening sections of part 1 include the headings "Ways of Coming to Know God" (CCC 31–35) and "The Knowledge of God according to the Church" (CCC 36–38). In these sections we find that there are "converging and convincing arguments" that "allow us to attain certainty about the truth" (CCC 31), and that "one can come to a knowledge of God as the origin and the end of the universe" (CCC 32). The *Catechism* reminds us that there are two "orders" of knowledge: (1) that which we can know through our own reasoning and (2) that which we know by faith, through God's revealing that which is beyond the grasp of our reason (see CCC 37 and Pius XII, *Humani Generis*, 561: DS 3875). Whether by reason or by faith, though, we are speaking always of the "knowability" of what is true and what is real.

At the same time, the *Catechism* reminds us that "God transcends all creatures" and that "[o]ur human words always fall short of the mystery of God" (CCC 42). It is because God is a mystery that there are many creeds that have been accepted by the Church. Obviously, these creeds do not contradict each other, but they do emphasize different points—one creed might concentrate on who Jesus is while another makes clearer what we believe about the Holy Spirit or the Church. The one Faith we have might be compared to the sun shining onto a prism—the creeds are like the many rays of color flowing out of it. There is no single way to describe a mystery.[1]

When the Church uses this word "mystery", then, she does not mean something that is unknowable by us, or something that seems blurred and unintelligible when we learn of it. The Church uses "mystery" as a way of referring to God himself and to his loving plan for us. The "mysteries of the Faith" are elements of this plan which God has revealed to us, and which we would not have known had God not revealed them.

It is important to maintain both of these positions. Only the conviction that the real is knowable allows us to proclaim the Faith at all, for if we cannot know God, but must be utterly agnostic, the necessity of Faith for our salvation becomes, literally, an unreasonable requirement (see CCC 154, 161). On the other hand, without a sense of God as mystery, always beyond the grasp of our minds, though not beyond their "touch", we conceive of God in too limited a way. The *Catechism* asks us to remember that "between Creator and creature no similitude can be expressed without implying an even greater dissimilitude" (CCC 43, citing Lateran Council IV: DS 806).

The loss of the true

That "the Faith is true" is a truism. Nonetheless, it is vital that this point is consciously acknowledged as part of God's pedagogy. Without this conviction, catechesis can be insufficiently explicit about the fact that our beliefs are true because they correspond to God's revelation of what is ultimately real. The role of the mind in knowing and in assenting to the real can then be underplayed.

---

[1] Because God transcends our words there will always be different expressions of his revelation. But of course there is also a common faith and a common language of faith and the creeds make use of this common language. Therefore, as Cardinal Ratzinger put it, what the *Catechism* aims to do "is to offer elements for a common basic language of faith" (*Gospel, Catechesis, Catechism* [San Francisco: Ignatius Press, 1997], p. 62).

Perhaps, as catechists, we can feel nervous when questions of truth are raised. This may be because truth implies the contrary possibility of error and falsity, and the rules of polite conversation typically rule out such categorical language. This in turn has an effect upon the ways in which we, as catechists, conceive of our role. Leading catechetical sessions, we are aware of the need to "listen to all points of view", to "respect all contributions", and to foster within our sessions an ethos of respectful listening. These are important points, but equally important points—concerning what to do about the proclamation and explanation of the Church's Faith precisely as true, and therefore worthy of assent—cannot be neglected. This would inevitably lead to a one-sided consideration of the catechist's role. Indeed it is stressed by many in catechetical circles that one should conceive of one's role as essentially that of facilitator rather than teacher, but this view is erroneous.

But what does one facilitate, if the catechist role is conceived in these terms? Normally, what is spoken of is "the sharing of experiences", or "faith-sharing". One of the difficulties of this approach lies in the ambiguities associated with the term "experience". As Cardinal Schönborn has noted,

> [W]hile it is clear that catechesis should refer to the lived experience of its hearers, its first responsibility or aim is to go beyond them towards what, by its very nature, does not form part of everyday experience. Faith takes us elsewhere. It opens up new unknown horizons, and in that way opens up space for experiences that everyday experience does not know. In theological terms: the faith is a response to an unheard-of revelation. Beginning from lived experience in the today of our young people we do not automatically arrive at revealed faith.[2]

We need briefly to consider, then, the role and importance of experience in catechesis, and especially the relationship of experience to truth. The *General Directory for Catechesis* offers us important guidance on this.

The *Directory* emphasizes that experience is a key "locus" for "the manifestation and realization of salvation". Here we can "assimilate" the "truths which constitute the objective content of Revelation" (GDC

---

[2] Christoph Cardinal Schönborn, "Address on 10th Anniversary of the Publication of the Catechism", October 2002, trans. Dudley Plunkett in *The Sower*, July 2003, p. 8.

152). The intellect does not work alone in the reception of revelation. The truths of the Faith can also be experienced because, as we have seen, the Faith is personal and we relate to it with the whole of who we are—our minds, emotions, bodies, and in and through the "heart", that deepest point within us (see CCC 2562). The *Catechism* speaks of the Holy Spirit "mobilizing the whole being" (CCC 1769). We saw in the previous chapter that the Faith is personal: propositions and concepts are rooted in *personal, living reality*. Because we are persons we are filled with an infinite thirst to know truth *as personal*, to know a Person. This knowing takes place in and through the whole of our being, including our experiences.

For this reason, the *Catechism* offers us numerous examples of lived Christian experiences through uniting the words and examples of the saints to the doctrines that are proposed. These hagiographical sources "have often been chosen with a view to direct catechetical use" (CCC 21). The saints exemplify for us authentic Christian experience, illustrating how one who loves God, and has faith and hope in him, responds to the difficulties in life, views creation, appreciates the beauties of the world, embraces the Church, and so on (see CCC 32, 313, 344, 826). To cite Cardinal Schönborn once more,

> [C]atechesis so urgently needs the example of Christian life and reference to lived Christian experience. It is from this experience above all that catechesis should begin, from the witness of the new life, of the happiness that it brings, of the visible and observable transformations that it produces. The *Catechism of the Catholic Church* seeks to encourage catechists to refer to Christian experience in often citing the saints of the Church.[3]

The *Directory* also emphasizes the need to unite experience and our critical faculties, using the "light of the Gospel" to assist us, so that we may be "educated" "in a new way of life" becoming "capable of behaving in a responsible and active way before the gift of God" (GDC 152). We are not to divide experience from the mind, as though there were two, separate ways here of approaching the Lord and receiving his revelation. Our minds and our way of living are to be renewed under the inspiration and guidance of the Holy Spirit (see Rom 12:2;

[3] Ibid., p. 9.

Gal 5:25). We then not only have faith in the interior enlightenment of the Holy Spirit, but also experience his strengthening of us to live as "children of light" (CCC 1695). Sensitive to the promptings of the Spirit, the mind assists in assimilating experiences, interpreting them and judging them in the light of the way of Christ.

The *Catechism* is asking us, then, to rediscover the Faith as true because it is real and to give the mind its proper place in catechesis, not isolated from experience, from affectivity, from the will, and from all that is richly personal, but as having an indispensable part to play in all catechesis.

Goodness

The *Catechism*, then, presents the Faith as both *one* and *true*. It also presents the Faith as *good*, as innately attractive and appealing to the human person. This is obviously of vital importance to us as catechists, since if we can help those we are catechizing to understand that the Faith points us to the source of true beatitude we are directly meeting the deepest desires of the heart. *The Heart Is a Lonely Hunter*, as the title of Carson McCuller's novel has it. But in the *Catechism* one finds the *Heart of God* revealed, and it is a Heart beating with love for his creation. And the merciful goodness of the heart of God fills the pages of the *Catechism*, underpinning and inspiring every section. One finds this presented in a rich variety of ways, all of which are given so that an assent *and adherence* of the whole person to the Faith can be supported, for we are evangelizing and catechizing effectively when the *will* and the *desires* of the heart, as well as the intellect, are engaged.

We can begin where the *Catechism* begins. Everyone is seeking happiness. This is the *Catechism's* starting point. As we noted earlier, in part 3 it quotes from St. Augustine, who wrote, "We all want to live happily; in the whole human race there is no one who does not assent to this proposition, even before it is fully articulated." [4] And it is because of the universal quest for happiness that it can speak confidently of the heart's yearning for God—because only in God can each person ultimately find that happiness (see CCC 27).

---

[4] CCC 1718, citing St. Augustine, *De moribus ecclesiae catholicae* 1, 3, 4; PL 32:1312.

God is the source of our happiness. "God alone satisfies." [5] The argument that this is the case, that nothing else can finally satisfy, is only alluded to in the *Catechism*, which is not a work of apologetics but of proclamation. But it indicates where to turn through the sources referred to—such as St. Augustine's *Confessions* and St. Thomas' *Summa*. And the *Catechism* expounds Christ's teaching on the route we must follow to reach such true happiness: the Beatitudes, it says, express "the paradoxical promises that sustain hope" (CCC 1717).

The question of human happiness, then, is a primary concern in the *Catechism*: it lies at the root of our understanding of the Faith as well as at the center of our motivation for living the moral life. Both the first and the third parts of the *Catechism* begin from this desire for happiness, and the task and joy of discovering that happiness in God. We are seeking for that which is our good, for that which will provide our fulfillment. The sense of the overwhelming generosity and goodness of God permeates the *Catechism*, as the ultimate answer to all of our searching. The *Catechism* is asking us, as catechists, to highlight the life-giving goodness of the Lord in our presentations of the Faith.

As we have noted, one of the key words in the description of the meaning of the logo, and elsewhere in the *Catechism*, is "draws". "God never ceases to draw man to himself" (CCC 27). This word emphasizes the work of grace in our lives, engaging the will. It helps us to be attentive to the ways in which God works to bring us to himself as the infinitely attractive goal of our lives. "Although man can forget God or reject him, [h]e never ceases to call every man to seek him, so as to find life and happiness" (CCC 30).

The *Catechism* follows St. Thomas in locating its treatment of grace, not within the treatment of the Faith in the first part, but in the section in the moral life. This is an important emphasis for us to consider in our teaching on the moral life that is so often understood as presented as a series of obligations for us to fulfill. The New Law, by which the Christian lives, is defined in the *Catechism* as "the *grace of the Holy Spirit*" (CCC 1966). The moral life is a life of grace, a life sustained and brought to perfection by the love of the Holy Spirit filling our hearts, purifying and converting us so that we can receive ever more fully all that God wants to give us—himself.

---

[5] CCC 1718, citing St. Thomas Aquinas, *Expos. in Symb. apost.* I.

Love, the passions, and the virtues

"The whole concern of doctrine and its teaching must be directed to the love that never ends" (CCC 25).[6] In everything that we teach the *Catechism* wants us to make explicit the love and goodness of God. We only understand any doctrine of the Faith rightly when we see it in this light.

Likewise, the *Catechism* says that we only understand the human person adequately when we appreciate that in man "the most fundamental passion is love, aroused by the attraction of the good" (CCC 1765). It is this fundamental passion of love that causes us to desire the good that we do not yet have, which causes us to yearn after our fulfillment. This "movement" of love within us, continues the *Catechism*, "finds completion in the pleasure and joy of the good possessed". The moral life consists in our cooperation with God's grace so that the passions are transformed into stable virtues, stable habits of living that are consistently responsive to God's good will.

Finally, let us remind ourselves once more that the-Faith-as-good that attracts us is identified as *personal*. At the center of the *Catechism* stands the figure of Christ, who alone is our life and the satisfaction of the good of the whole person. We are drawn by an incarnate, enfleshed love, so as to know and enjoy as our eternal good the life of the Blessed Trinity. Over and again the *Catechism* reiterates that at the center of catechesis must be the Person of Christ—not only because he is the supreme revealer and teacher, but also because he is our incarnate good. Lifted up from the earth he draws all men to himself.

And when we say that Christ draws us, we mean "*Christus totus*", the "whole Christ", which is Christ and his Church: "Do you understand and grasp, brethren, God's grace toward us? Marvel and rejoice: we have become Christ." [7]

And so the *Catechism* also pays a good deal of attention to the saints, and especially our Lady. The sections of the *Catechism* invariably conclude with citations and examples from the saints, illustrating the culminating glory of the Faith and its best demonstration. The saints, who have been attracted by the love and goodness of God, participate in that same drawing of all things into divine joy. As Gerard Manley

---

[6] Citing here the *Roman Catechism*, Preface, 10; cf. 1 Cor 13:8.
[7] CCC 795, citing St. Augustine, *In Jo. ev.* 21, 8; PL 35:1568.

Hopkins put it, "for Christ plays in ten thousand places, / Lovely in limbs, and lovely in eyes not his".[8] Or, rather, the eyes that draw us into everlasting life are always his, for we belong to him.

Beauty

When we come to consider the fourth of the transcendental properties of Being, beauty, we need to pause in order to emphasize the Catholic understanding that beauty is an objective aspect of what is real. Beauty is not simply in the eye of the beholder, any more than truth is only in the mind or goodness a mere personal preference. Beauty is the "radiance of Being": the more any particular creature is unified, good, and true, to that extent the creature is more beautiful.

Dante writes of the value of beauty in its ability to draw one toward meaning. He imagines one of his poems speaking to a reader who cannot understand its meaning: "If you cannot see my goodness, at least attend to my beauty. Which is to say ... O you who cannot see the meaning of this song, do not reject it on that account; only look at its beauty, which is great",[9] and he goes on to speak of the song's sentence construction, organization, and the relation of the parts to the whole, its order.

The theme of a natural attraction through sensible beauty to rational order recurs in Dante's *Divine Comedy*. Dante describes this attracting power of the order of the universe: "The high heavens call you and about you wheel, showing eternal beauties to invite you."[10] In a wonderful passage in the *Paradiso* Dante summarizes his presentation of God's design in drawing to himself, as the eternal beauty, created minds through the beauties of creation and the order that he has set in the universe:

> The primal ineffable Power made with such order
> all that circles through mind or space
> that he who contemplates it cannot but taste of him.

[8] *Poems of Gerard Manley Hopkins*, Third ed. (New York: Oxford University Press, 1948), no. 57, p. 95.
[9] *Convivio* 2, 11.
[10] *Purgatorio* XIV, 148–49.

> Lift up, then, reader, with me your eyes to the great wheels,
> directing them on that point where one motion strikes on
>   the other,
> and there begin to delight in the art of the Master
> who so loves it in himself that his eye never leaves it.[11]

We find that the link between sensible beauty and order is indicated also in the *Catechism* (CCC 32). The *Catechism* may surprise us, in fact, in the emphasis it places on the beauty and the intrinsic attractiveness of the Faith. Look at these phrases that Pope John Paul II used to speak about the Faith in his introduction to the *Catechism, Fidei Depositum*:

> The Second Vatican Ecumenical Council ... had as its intention and purpose to highlight the Church's apostolic and pastoral mission and by making the truth of the Gospel *shine forth* to lead all people to seek and receive Christ's love which surpasses all knowledge (cf. Eph 3:19)....
>   [T]he Council was not first of all to condemn the errors of the time, but above all to *strive calmly to show the strength and beauty of the doctrine of the faith.* "*Illumined* by the light of this Council", the Pope said, "the Church ... will become greater in spiritual riches."[12]

Notice the important connections being established between the truth of the Faith and its beauty. It is not enough to seek and to teach what is true. We must also be aware of the power of the Faith to attract us by its beauty. The truth is to "shine forth". We are to strive calmly to show how *beautiful* doctrine is.

The *Catechism* identifies four specific ways in which the beauty of the Faith can be brought out.

First, *that the Faith is beautiful is made most evident by the beauty of the lives of Christians*: "In order that the message of salvation can show the power of its truth and *radiance* before men, it must be authenticated by the witness of the life of Christians" (CCC 2044; emphasis added). Most of us are drawn to the Faith and to an initial or a deeper conversion to Christ through meeting Christians who radiate the loveliness of Christ in their lives. "This spiritual beauty of God is reflected in the most holy Virgin Mother of God, the angels, and saints" (CCC

---

[11] *Paradiso* X, 3–12.
[12] CCC, pp. 1–2, emphasis added.

2502; see also 1701). The serene, prayerful, and joyful catechist is the best witness to the truth of the Faith. "The practice of goodness is accompanied by spontaneous spiritual joy and moral beauty" (CCC 2500).

Second, "*Truth is beautiful in itself*" (CCC 2500). Truth is beautiful because all Being is beautiful and is a reflection of the One who is beauty himself. "The beauty of creation reflects the infinite beauty of the Creator and ought to inspire the respect and submission of man's intellect and will" (CCC 341). The *Catechism* quotes St. Augustine on this point. In the section on evidence for the existence of God, the *Catechism* teaches:

> St. Augustine issues this challenge: Question the beauty of the earth, question the beauty of the sea, question the beauty of the air distending and diffusing itself, question the beauty of the sky ... question all these realities. All respond: "See, we are beautiful." Their beauty is a profession [*confessio*]. These beauties are subject to change. Who made them if not the Beautiful One [*Pulcher*] who is not subject to change?[13]

Third, *art, and especially explicitly Christian art—sacred art—can lead people to appreciate the beauty of the Faith* (see CCC 2501–2). The point is reinforced for us by the insistence of the authors that works of Christian art appear in the *Catechism*, placed at the beginning of each part. It is a timely reminder for us that catechesis was, for many centuries, conducted primarily through a variety of art forms—stained-glass windows, the architecture of churches, sacred music, and the making of icons and other forms of Christian art. The *Catechism* is calling us to rediscover the importance of these for an authentic Christian catechesis, one which not only informs our students about the Faith but also attracts them to it.

Fourth, *prayer is defined as* "the 'love of beauty' (*philokalia*)" (CCC 2727). Prayer is the love of beauty because it is the direct relationship of the person with the One who is All-beautiful, and therefore in prayer one is "caught up in the glory of the living and true God" (ibid.). In prayer, like Mary, one opens oneself to be the "place where the glory of the Lord dwells" (CCC 2676): one models oneself upon Mary, full of grace, who "is wholly given over to him who has come to dwell in her" (ibid.).

---

[13] CCC 32, citing St. Augustion, *Sermo* 241, 2; PL 38:1134.

Having now considered the significance of the transcendentals of Being in the proclamation of the Faith in the *Catechism* we can formulate two further keys.

KEY 5 TRUE

We proclaim the mysteries of the Faith as true, as realities that we can *truly* know, though never know *fully*.

KEY 6 ATTRACTIVE

We highlight the innately attractive nature of the Faith through using the beauty of nature and art and examples drawn from the joyful witness of those who have found their happiness in God.

Chapter Five

A Purposeful Pedagogy:
Teaching the Story of Salvation

This chapter examines the centrality of what we can call "the Story of Salvation" in the craft of catechesis. This is the story of God's loving plan of redemption, carried out in history through the joint mission of the Son and Holy Spirit.

We have already seen that the life and plan of the Blessed Trinity lie at the heart of the pedagogy of God. This is the center of catechesis. We cited earlier one of the most important paragraphs in the *Catechism*, which speaks of the Trinity being the "central mystery" of both "Christian faith and life" (CCC 234). This paragraph concludes with the statement: "The whole history of salvation is identical with the history of the way and the means by which the one true God, Father, Son, and Holy Spirit, reveals himself to men 'and reconciles and unites with himself those who turn away from sin'."[1] The history of salvation, then, is nothing other than the history of the Blessed Trinity's revelation of himself in order to reconcile us to him (see 2 Cor 5:19). Catechesis finds in this plan its unwavering purpose. The history of salvation is told and handed on to enable everyone to understand God's purpose in revealing himself in words and deeds: to bring us to share eternal happiness with him in heaven.

The basic outline of this plan, of the Story of Salvation, is given for us in CCC 54–73. As catechists we need to know this story well and be able to communicate it to others. It is the context within which we can place our teaching on all other matters. Cardinal Schönborn has written:

---

[1] CCC 234, citing GDC 47.

It is of the greatest importance once more to speak of God's plan. The great model for this is the liturgical anamnesis. It places our life and our time within the perspective of God's merciful plan. We must dare to proclaim this great plan of God in a coherent way. . . . The Credo, the Symbol of the Apostles, the basis for the first part of the *Catechism*, gives us a good example. It is not without reason that catechumens first receive the Symbol of the faith which contains a summary of the whole of the plan of God. In welcoming the Symbol of the faith we also receive our place in this history, in this great drama of God's plan, and we find our place in the history of salvation. And we see that here is a new history, different from that which the world teaches us, and which we used to think was our history.[2]

We need to be able to speak of God's plan, to tell this story both in outline and also in more detail, as the need arises; we need to be able to tell it briefly and more extensively; at the beginning of sessions, to provide the context for what follows, and at the conclusion, to sum up what has gone before; in a form suitable for children and in an appropriate manner for adults; using art to illustrate it and using stories to accompany it; for the sake of understanding the past, for interpreting the present, and for preparing for the future:

The Church, in transmitting today the Christian message . . . has a constant memory of the saving events of the past and makes them known. In the light of these, she interprets the present events of human history, where the Spirit of God is continually renewing the face of the earth, and she waits with faith for the Lord's coming.[3]

From the beginning

In the transmission of the Faith, then, we are advised to look to the "constant memory" of the Church and her recalling of the "wonderful works of God", and in particular "the work of Christ the Lord in redeeming mankind and giving perfect glory to God".[4] All of God's works have one and the same vital purpose: they are to bring us to

[2] Christoph Cardinal Schönborn, "Address on 10th Anniversary of the Publication of the Catechism", October 2002, trans. Dudley Plunkett in *The Sower*, July 2003, p. 9.
[3] GDC 107.
[4] CCC 1067, citing SC 5 no. 2; cf. St. Augustine, *En. in. Ps.* 138, 2; PL 37:1784–85.

conversion for the sake of eternal happiness. In the life of the ancient people of God, therefore, we find a strong theme to be that of recalling the great works of God:

> We will not hide them from their children,
> but tell to the coming generation
> the glorious deeds of the LORD,
> and his might,
> and the wonders which he has wrought.[5]

From the earliest times in the Church, then, we find that an essential part of catechesis has been recalling for others the story of creation and salvation. We find one of the first instances in the Gospel of St. Luke. As we have already mentioned, Luke 24:13–35 gives the account of two of the disciples walking out from Jerusalem after the Passion and death of the Lord. On their journey they are met by an apparent stranger who walks alongside them. The stranger explains to them how the Scriptures contain the key to a deeper understanding of the recent events they were pondering, once these events have been correctly interpreted. The disciples ask the stranger to remain with them and recognize him as Christ at the breaking of bread.

This story of the disciples meeting the Risen Christ on the road to Emmaus has been a popular one in guiding thinking about catechetical methodology. What can it tell us about the work of catechesis, and in particular about the significance of telling of the story of salvation?[6]

---

[5] Ps 78:4; see also Ps 105, 136.

[6] The Emmaus image is often used to support a catechetical approach in which people are first of all invited to "share their story" with the catechist and with others being catechized. The emphasis is placed on the need to listen to what those we are catechizing have to say about their own experiences and ideas. Only after they have done this, it is sometimes suggested, should the catechist speak Christ's word into their situation. We need to focus on the actual Gospel text in order to see whether this is the most accurate understanding of the story. In fact it is important to note, first of all, that the "story" we are concerned with is that of Jesus' Passion. The Emmaus account does not yield a general encouragement to others to "tell their story" so much as a specific invitation to focus on *how we understand Jesus' death and Resurrection*. Further, Jesus' rebuff of the disciples should warn us to be careful: "O foolish men, and slow of heart to believe all that the prophets have spoken!" (24:25). Here is no gentle response to the telling of the disciples' story, but a sharp rejoinder and an evaluation of the inadequacy of their "story", their account of Jesus' Passion. Jesus listens, and it is vital that as catechists we listen. But *how* we listen and what we listen *for* is also very important. Jesus listens for faith, hope, and love in the telling

First of all, we are offered here an image of the Christian life as a
journey in which there is a fundamental movement from doubt to
faith, from confusion to conviction. St. Luke twice uses the phrase
that the disciples were "on the way" (Lk 24:32, 35; New American
Bible), an allusion to the name given to Christians in the early decades,
"Followers of the Way" (Acts 19:23; 22:4; 24:22). We have here an
early story, then, of how one is moved from doubt to faith on the
Christian "Way".

Secondly, the story of Emmaus stresses that Christ is often unrec-
ognized on this journey, that a spiritual awakening is required in order
to see him. There is a need to be born "from above" (Jn 3:3), for the
"eyes" of the heart (see Eph 1:18) to be opened. This movement from
doubt to faith, of the awakening of the inner sight of the disciples,
takes place through two related activities:

- In the first place, Jesus, the stranger, *proclaims the Story of Salvation*. The Emmaus account is concerned to emphasize Jesus'
  role as teacher and interpreter of the Scriptures: "And beginning with Moses and all the prophets, he interpreted to them
  in all the Scriptures the things concerning himself" (Lk 24:27).
  Jesus tells them the Story of Salvation, with himself as the center and interpretative key. It is clear from the passage that it is
  indeed *every part* of the Scriptures that he interpreted (see 24:44).
  We can learn from this passage how important it is for us, as
  catechists, to be able to identify the Christ-centered nature
  and significance of the Old Testament, and the way in which
  Jesus is the fulfillment of all of the promises of God (see CCC
  122). The two disciples are able to recall the last few days of
  the story but their lack of faith is in part because they are
  unable to interpret the meaning of the segment they have in

---

of the story and, hearing the confusion and despair of the disciples, he speaks in order to
bring them back to the truth, and to reenkindle their faith and hope. We should also be
cautious about any suggestion that the road to Emmaus account encourages us to concentrate upon others telling their story to the detriment of the Church telling hers: rather,
God has entrusted the Church with the revelation of his story, and she exists in order to
communicate this to others. For an account of the meaning of the Emmaus story consistent with the way we have interpreted it here, see Eugene Kevane, *Jesus the Divine Teacher:
Fullness and Mediator of Biblical Revelation* (New York: Vantage Press, 2003), pp. 213–214.

the light of the whole story. The small part that they know does not, by itself, make sense to them. This whole story is what Jesus now proclaims (see Lk 24:27).[7]

- In the second place, the moment of recognition, of spiritual awakening, comes with the *"breaking of the bread"*. It is then that the disciples are able to reflect upon their earlier cate-chesis and know that their hearts were, even then, "burning" within them. We know that the phrase "breaking of the bread" was an early name given to the Eucharist (CCC 1329). The Emmaus story clearly uses Eucharistic language: Christ "took", "blessed", "broke", and "gave". In the Emmaus story, then, we have a clear "echo" of the two parts of the Eucharist, with the "breaking open" of the Word being fol-lowed by the breaking of bread. The Scriptures are inter-preted within the context of the liturgy (see CCC 1347). It is within the liturgy, in particular, that we shall hear the Story of Salvation.

This appearance of Jesus to the disciples under the form of bread and through the telling of the Story of Salvation concludes with this strik-ing verse: "And they rose that same hour and returned to Jerusalem" (24:33). The drawing together of the language of resurrection ("they rose", *anastantes*), "the hour"—recalling the "hour" of the Passion—and the disciples' return to Jerusalem, echoing the appearance of the Risen Christ in Jerusalem, bears testimony to the importance of this account in St. Luke's Gospel: here is the moment of spiritual resur-rection, through the insertion of the disciples, in and through the Eucha-rist, into the "hour" of Christ's Paschal mystery, so that they return to Jerusalem with the Risen Lord and can appear with the good news to the other disciples.

---

[7] The Emmaus story is paralleled in the Acts of the Apostles by the account of Philip meeting with the Ethiopian eunuch (Acts 8:26–40). Here again is a request to have the Scriptures explained: "How can I understand [/] unless some one guides me?" (v. 31). Philip shows how the Scriptures find their fulfillment in the life, death, and Resurrection of Christ, and the Ethiopian is baptized. In this parallel account, then, it is clear that the author of Luke-Acts is telling us that the Church has the authority to teach the true interpretation of the Scriptures. Catechists have received through the Church their own delegated authority to teach Christ's truth.

The *narratio*

We can see from this early account the importance of the proclamation of the Story of Salvation, centered on Christ, in the Church's catechesis. The Church called this Story of Salvation the *"narratio"*, or "narration".[8] It is the narrative of the Faith. It is the Deposit of Faith proclaimed as truths discovered within the living history of the People of God.

The *General Directory for Catechesis* speaks of seven "foundation stones" or "basic elements" that lie at the heart of catechesis. We find all of them in the *Catechism*. Four of these foundation stones are the four parts of the *Catechism*. As we know, these four parts correspond to the four dimensions of the Christian life: "The Profession of Faith" (part 1); "The Celebration of the Christian Mystery" (part 2); "Life in Christ" (part 3); "Christian Prayer" (part 4). These are the four "pillars" of the Christian life: we believe, worship, live, and pray.

The other three foundation stones are "the three phases in the narration of the history of salvation" (GDC 130): the Old Testament, the life of Jesus, and the history of the Church. The *General Directory for Catechesis* asks us to set our expositions of the faith, life, and worship of the Church *within* this narrative framework. In other words, when we catechize and explain the truths of Catholic faith and life we are helping our hearers to understand these truths as *elements within the Story of Salvation*.

This catechesis is intensely *purposeful*—it brings to the fore the dynamic sense of divine intelligence and purpose underlying our own lives, the lives of our hearers, and the whole of creation. This truth is affirmed in numerous places in the *Catechism*, and it is an important element for us to highlight when using images of discipleship and journeying.[9] Thus, for instance, we read that "the universe was created

---

[8] We find the narration highlighted, for example, in St. Augustine's work on catechesis, *De Catechizandis Rudibus*, Ancient Christian Writers Series (London: Westminster, 1946). For a discussion of the importance of the *narratio* in the catechesis of the early Church, focusing especially on the work of St. Irenaeus, see Andrew Minto, "How the Divine Pedagogy Teaches", *The Sower* 25, no. 4 (2003): 6–8.

[9] This focus on the *end* or *purpose* of the journey enables us to avoid any unintentional reception of the image of the Christian journey as merely endless "wandering". The punishment of the people of Israel when they disobeyed the Lord and could not enter the Promised Land meant precisely a turning away from their "end", the land "flowing with milk and honey", and a "journey into the wilderness" (Deut 1:40). Even so, this takes place under the Lord's protection (Deut 2:7), and for only a limited period, to exorcise the

'in a state of journeying' (*in statu viae*) toward an ultimate perfection yet to be attained, to which God has destined it." [10]

Catechesis lives from the spiritual joy of *the certainty of the end*, which is that of sharing in the beatitude of the life of the Trinity (see CCC 1721): "Faith is the assurance of things hoped for, the conviction of things not seen" (Heb 11:1). Catechesis, therefore, begins from the end, for this is where faith is rooted—in our final destiny—and speaks with the confidence of the children of God that accompanies this, a confidence (in Greek, *parrhesia*) beautifully described in the *Catechism* as "straightforward simplicity, filial trust, joyous assurance, humble boldness, the certainty of being loved".[11]

The *Catechism* often points us to the need to understand the beginning of the story and its progress *in the light of the end of the story*. We can understand why this is so by reflecting on living processes in the natural world: G. K. Chesterton wrote, "If seeds in the black earth can turn into such beautiful roses, what might not the heart of man become in its long journey toward the stars?"[12] We see the beauty of a seed when it has flowered into a magnificent red rose. When the rosebush finally brings forth its roses we can see the significance, the point, of the seed falling into the earth and remaining hidden for many months, and of the plant being patiently tended and cared for. This point of analogy between the story of salvation and living, created things can remind us that the *purposefulness of doctrine* is one aspect implied in its description as "organic", living. All living things have a *telos*, an end, and it is this end which directs the striving and activity of every living creature. All creatures aim for what they consider their fulfillment, their final good. It can also help us, as catechists, to contemplate the future glory of the seeds being planted through the work of catechesis. Seeds apparently disappearing into black earth have their *telos*, their end, in the beauty of heaven.

What is true of the rose is true of creation as a whole. Christ "casts conclusive light" on creation and "reveals the end" for which creation

---

spirit of distrust from the people. In the Christian dispensation, all journeying is a "pilgrimage", a movement toward that which is holy, "no longer merely to the possession of a territory, but to the Kingdom of heaven" (CCC 1716).

[10] CCC 302.

[11] CCC 2778; cf. Eph 3:12; Heb 3:6; 4:16; 10:19; 1 Jn 2:28; 3:21; 5:14.

[12] Maisie Ward, *Return to Chesterton* (London, 1952), p. 137.

is intended, and so catechists can helpfully focus on "the glory of the new creation in Christ", the final point of the pain and struggle over the millennia during which the beauties of the created order have evolved: we then realize that what we are seeing at the moment is the gradual growth of the "seed" as it is drawn upward toward the light and the sun (see CCC 280).

"The two questions, the first about the origin and the second about the end, are inseparable" (CCC 282). In the light of revelation, we know that the origin and the end point in a single direction. The story has love as its source, its driving force, and its goal. The origin and end are also "decisive for the meaning and orientation of our life and actions" (CCC 282), which is why "[t]he beatitude we are promised confronts us with decisive moral choices" (CCC 1723). Telling the *narratio*, therefore, enables a proper focus on the end, which in turn provides a key for *understanding both doctrine and life*.

As we have seen, the story is grounded in the life of the Trinity, who 'reconciles and unites with himself those who turn away from sin'."[13] Like all good stories, the *narratio* has a beginning, middle, and end. The beginning is the act of creation. The middle and center-point is the coming among us, "beyond all expectation" (CCC 422), of the Son of God, his Incarnation, life, death, and Resurrection. The end of the story is the second coming of Christ, which ushers in the four "last things" for the whole of humanity: death, judgment, heaven, and hell. These give us the key marker points in the *narratio*. They tell us where we must start and finish and where the story reaches its central climax—in the redemptive life and work of Christ. The *General Directory for Catechesis* describes the main sections of the story, through which God has revealed himself to us, as

> the great stages of the Old Testament by which God prepared the journey of the Gospel; the life of Jesus, Son of God, born of the Virgin Mary, who by his actions and teaching brought Revelation to completion; the history of the Church which transmits Revelation.[14]

In synthetic form, of course, the *narratio* is proclaimed in the creeds of the Church. These creeds are trinitarian in structure:

[13] CCC 234, citing GDC 47.
[14] GDC 108.

[T]he first part speaks of the first divine Person and the wonderful work of creation; the next speaks of the second divine Person and the mystery of his redemption of men; the final part speaks of the third divine Person, the origin and source of our sanctification.[15]

Reflecting this creedal structure and *narratio*, the *Catechism* organizes doctrinal material to reflect this dynamic of God's merciful plan. The material is related to the three Persons of the Trinity and to the three principal works of the Persons. As we saw above, the first period is the time of the Father, whose principal work is creation; the second era is the time of the Son, whose work is redemption, while the third era is the time of the Holy Spirit, and also the age of the Church, the new People of God, since the primary work of the Holy Spirit is sanctification (for example, see CCC 1076, in which the gift of the Spirit at Pentecost is said to usher in a "new era").[16]

The whole of the creedal section in part 1 of the *Catechism* is, obviously enough, organized in this way, and we see it reflected also in the opening of part 4, on Christian prayer, which introduces us to the call to prayer in three consecutive periods: "in the Old Testament" (CCC 2568–97), "in the fullness of time" (CCC 2598–2622), and "in the age of the Church" (CCC 2623–49).

In addition to whole parts of the *Catechism* presenting doctrinal content in and through the *narratio*, we find that this characterizes the treatment of individual topics and sections. Thus, for example, the *Catechism* lovingly presents its teaching on the Church as a meditation on "her origin in the Holy Trinity's plan and her progressive realization in history" (CCC 758). This meditation locates the Church as "a plan born in the Father's heart" (CCC 759), traces her institution in Christ "in the fullness of time" (CCC 763), and looks forward to her perfection in "the glory of heaven" (CCC 769, citing LG 48).

The treatment of the sacraments, similarly, typically begins from a contemplation of each sacrament within the framework of the "economy of salvation", the plan of God (for example, see CCC 1217–28 on baptism, CCC 1286–92 on confirmation, and CCC 1333–44 on

---

[15] *Roman Catechism* I, 1, 3; cited in CCC 190.

[16] CCC 257–58 cautions us to remember that, while we speak in a human way of certain Persons of the Trinity being more associated with particular "works", at the same time: "The whole divine economy is the common work of the three divine persons."

the Eucharist). Only then does the *Catechism* begin a liturgical catechesis from the signs and rites associated with the sacraments in question. So common, in fact, is this use of the structure of the *narratio* to
articulate doctrine that individual paragraphs echo this format. So, for
instance, the *Catechism*'s explanation of the word "*daily*" (*epiousios*)
from the Lord's Prayer begins with its meaning in the time of the Old
Covenant then moves on to examine it by reference to the life and
teaching of Christ, and finally indicates its meaning in the light of
"the feast of the kingdom" to come (see CCC 2837). The catechesis
on the names of the second Divine Person—"Jesus", "Christ", "Son
of God", and "Lord"—follows a similar movement through the "stages"
of salvation history (see CCC 759). Thus the *Catechism* models for us
the setting of our teaching within the *narratio*.

Finding ourselves in the *narratio*

Catechesis, then, proclaims "the mystery", the great overarching *exitus–*
reditus, which is the story of creation and redemption. This is the
story to which each of us belongs; it is, in the most profound sense,
our "family" story since, as the *Catechism* says, "There is a *solidarity*
among all creatures arising from the fact that all have the same Creator
and are all ordered to his glory" (CCC 344). Within this family of
creatures, the human family "*forms a unity*" (CCC 360), sharing as it
does the same origin, nature, and goal. Catechesis concerns that which
is *common to all people*. We are each of us created by God, bearing an
immortal soul and fundamentally equal in his sight. We are fallen,
corrupted, sinful, addicted to vice, and in need of healing grace. We
are redeemed by Christ and each of us is given the vocation to love
God with our whole hearts, souls, and strength. We have one nature,
one origin, and one calling, and the struggles in which we share are
struggles common to us all. Catechesis is the annunciation of these
supreme truths of creation, redemption, and sanctification. Everything
in the *Catechism* is for each person. As we know, "Catholic" means
"universal" (CCC 830) and catechesis involves the transmission of a
universal message of salvation in Jesus Christ, who took "human nature"
at the Incarnation, who died for the salvation of all, and who has a
message and a mission for all races and all generations to the ends of

the earth and the end of time. Our work of catechesis has a universal relevance precisely because of this common *narratio*.[17] We announce these truths so that each person, with his own unique "life story", may find his deepest identity within the context of the *narratio*. It is helpful, therefore, to recount the story using "our", "we", and "us" to make it clear that it really is the story of every person.

KEY 7 PURPOSE

We immerse doctrine within the *narratio*, the dynamic history of God's plan and purpose for our salvation, within which the "narrative" of every life can find its true meaning.

[17] Early critics of the *Catechism* focused on the alleged impossibility of a single text for the whole of humanity in all its diverse cultures and races. According to Michael Walsh, "One of the most serious objections launched against the *Catechism* by its critics ... is that it is impossible to produce for so diverse a world a Catechism which is equally intelligible to all, and equally applicable around the globe" (*Commentary on the Catechism* [London: Geoffrey Chapman, 1992], p. 2). A single message of revelation is a problem for the critics precisely because of the diversity of man considered in his cultural settings. What is often lost or rejected by such critics is a sense of human nature that is common to all and therefore of a message that *can* relate to all.

Chapter Six

A Practical Pedagogy:
Identifying and Selecting Teaching Points

As catechists, we often face difficult decisions when planning our teaching. As we seek to plan each suitable and faithful catechetical session we have to ask the following questions: How do I identify and select my key teaching points? How much should I include in this session? What are the "most important" things that must be taught? How do I know whether I am choosing the "right" things? How can I be sure that I have not left out anything vital? If you are used to teaching a subject in three sessions and the parish priest asks you suddenly to teach it in one session instead, how do you select what to cover? If you have only one hour to teach on our Lady, what must you cover? What must you not leave out? We are often in a position where everything feels essential to us, but at the same time we know that the constraints of time prevent us from teaching everything.

In the life of one of the Church's greatest missionaries, St. Francis Xavier, we can see the same questions being raised: So much to teach . . . so little time . . . how can one select? St. Francis did manage to select:

> There was no time for careful teaching, for long instruction. On his arrival at a hamlet he would call together men and boys; in his halting, parrot-like Tamil he recited the Creed, the Commandments, some prayers, which he made his audience repeat after him when he had taught them to make the sign of the Cross. A question followed each article of the Creed: "Do you believe?" A murmur of many voices answered, as dusky arms were crossed on naked breasts: "We believe." Then came baptism and each new Christian received a palm-leaf on which the Father's own hand had written his Christian name.[1]

[1] Margaret Yeo, *St. Francis Xavier: Apostle to the East* (New York: MacMillan Company, 1932), p. 145.

What criteria are there for helping us to identify and select teaching points? Can the *Catechism of the Catholic Church* help in these areas?

The short answer is that the *Catechism* can indeed help us here. It has been written to assist us in the identification and selection of teaching points, and in this chapter we will examine how this practical help is provided.

We need to begin with a reminder of the doctrine of "Divine Simplicity". The Church teaches that God is "simple". This does *not* mean that God is comprehensible; we know, on the contrary, that he is ultimately mystery. The doctrine of God's simplicity means that he is without parts, without complexity (from the Latin *simplex—seme-plex—* single fold or one fold). God is the "one thing" necessary; he is pure unity, entirely straightforward. The material world is complex, made up of many parts; God is one. The *Catechism* speaks briefly of this doctrine in CCC 271, when it quotes from St. Thomas, who says, "In God, power, essence, will, intellect, wisdom, and justice are all identical." [2] We experience and learn about these realities as separate from each other, even in apparent opposition to each other. But in God they are all the same.

This doctrine of the Church helps us into the thought that although we sometimes imagine that the world around us is easy to understand, whereas the Church's Faith is complex and difficult, it is really the other way around. The gospel taught by Christ is actually startlingly straightforward and simple: God is your Father; be perfect; forgive your enemies; do not be anxious—the birds of the air do not worry; take up your cross; follow me; eat my flesh.

As catechists we can remember to locate ourselves always in the context of gospel simplicity. God is "simple", and Christ taught with the utmost simplicity because he was teaching about God. All the core truths of the Faith can be articulated with a simplicity suitable for children as well as for adults. Jesus said that unless his followers became like little children, they could not enter the kingdom of heaven (Mt 18:3). Little children can receive the gospel and respond to it in faith and in their lives. Our deepest mysteries can be taught to our youngest members. For example, we can use the sign of the cross to teach the mysteries of the Trinity, the redemption brought to us by

---

[2] CCC 271, citing St. Thomas Aquinas, ST I, 25, 5 ad 1.

the incarnate Son, and our own extraordinary dignity as children of the Father, called to share in the vocation of the Son.

We begin our consideration of this question of identifying and selecting key teaching points, then, by reminding ourselves of the doctrine of divine simplicity: we are seeking always to announce the saving doctrine of the Church in a simple, straightforward way. This can be done because doctrine *is* simple; and it is simple because it reflects *God's* simplicity.

The essentials of doctrine

The *Catechism* is a presentation of "the essential and fundamental contents of Catholic doctrine" (CCC 11). Clearly, everything in the *Catechism* is "essential" for us to teach: this is the doctrine that must be handed on. But, as we have seen, it is equally clear that it is not possible to teach this "everything" in a single session. A selection from the essentials of doctrine must be made in any particular session.

The term "essential" provides indications for us as to how this can be done. "Essential" comes from the word "essence", which specifies a thing's identity and meaning. We will be discovering in this chapter that the secret of the selection of teaching points is concerned with these two things: discovering the *identity* of a doctrine, or teaching, and discovering its *meaning*. In order to teach the Faith, the catechist can learn to discover from the *Catechism* the *identity* and *meaning* of each topic. Some examples will help us to understand what is required here.

Imagine that you are walking in the countryside. As you come over the top of a rise on your walk you see something in the distance. At this point you see that there is *something*, but cannot be sure *what* it is. You strain your eyes—is it a horse or a cow or just a small, squat building? You are trying to discern *essence* in the sense of its *identity*; you are trying to see what it is. Gradually you separate out the individual characteristics you see—its size, shape, whether it is moving, its color, and then you discern that it is in fact a cow standing very still. The essentials of doctrine have to do with the core identity of those doctrines.

Essence is also concerned with the *meaning*, or significance, of things. Again, let us take an example. If one walks into a busy hospital one will be aware of crowds of hurrying people, each carrying out a variety of tasks. But it is possible to stand back from the bustle and ask the question "What are they all concerned with? What is a hospital for?" When one has found the answer that a hospital is concerned with the care and healing of the sick one has found the "essence" of a hospital: this is what it is essential to know in order to make sense of all of the other activities taking place.[3] Finding the meaning of something, then, is vital for providing one with an overall perspective. It enables one to understand all of the other elements of that object.

Identifying and selecting teaching points for *identity*

It is obvious that we cannot select our teaching points simply in the light of our own preferences. We cannot make our decisions according to the criterion of what we find most attractive or compelling. This would leave us in danger of what John Paul has described as the "mutilation" of the Faith. He wrote, "The person who becomes a disciple of Christ has the right to receive "the word of faith" not in mutilated, falsified or diminished form but whole and entire, in all its rigor and vigor."[4]

We clearly need objective criteria for the selection of our key teaching points that will ensure that we hand on the "word of faith" "whole and entire". In other words, the selection of teaching points is never just a reflection of what the catechist himself believes is important or unimportant. When we base our selection of the essentials of doctrine upon our own opinions we risk leaving those we are catechizing with an incomplete understanding of that doctrine.

We will, of course, know how important it is to take into account the needs of the audience when we are selecting the key teaching points related to any topic. *The General Directory for Catechesis* reminds us of the importance of the principle of "Fidelity to God and to the person" (GDC 145) when catechizing according to the pedagogy of

---

[3] For this example, we are indebted to Robert Sokolowski, *Introduction to Phenomenology* (Cambridge, Eng.: Cambridge University Press, 1999).

[4] CT 30, citing Rom 10:8.

God. "Fidelity to the person" means that the selection of what to teach from the Deposit of Faith for any given audience must take into account, not only the amount of time available, but also such factors as age, education, background, and culture. We ought also to bear in mind any areas in which there are common misunderstandings. Points that in one culture might be omitted can in another be essential to make. For example, in many Western cultures, exposure to New Age thinking can mean that there is a tendency to overemphasize the immanence of God as well as the view that religion has a mainly therapeutic role and is an aid to self-empowerment and self-actualization. Distinguishing the Faith from these emphases is important: knowing what the Church does *not* teach can help one to be clearer what she *does* teach about a particular doctrine or practice. In many African cultures, by comparison, it can be particularly important to stress the omnipotent nature of God and the absolute distinction between the power of God and that of other "spirits".

Given that we will be taking these issues into account, let us look at the guidance that the *Catechism* provides for us in our selection of teaching points for any topic. Let us take one section as an example: God as "The Almighty" (see CCC 268–78). How does the *Catechism* assist us in selecting teaching points?

The first point to note is the divisions of the section. We see that there are three bold *subheadings*, prefaced by an introductory paragraph. We might guess—and we would be correct—that there are three main points being taught in this section about the almighty nature of God. The structure, and then the number of paragraphs, is an important guide to how many key points are being taught.

Second, if we then look at the introductory paragraph to this topic, CCC 268, we will note that there are three italicized words there: "*universal*", "*loving*", and "*mysterious*". The *Catechism* is telling us what the three essential points are in its teaching on this subject. (We can confirm this by a careful reading of the paragraphs under each subheading.)

Subheadings and the use of italics in the text are two important helps that the authors of the *Catechism* have provided in order to assist us in our selection. At this point, we can be attentive also to what seem to be points of emphasis, where the authors are highlighting the importance of a particular idea. It is worth noting key phrases indicated by words such as "important" or "fundamental", or words that recur frequently. In CCC 268, for instance, we can note the phrase "great bearing", which alerts us to the fact that something highly significant for the understanding of the subject is being announced.

Two further points to note here are as follows:

- *Each key teaching point is expanded* and supported by numerous references and texts from Scripture and Tradition. For example, CCC 269 begins to fill out the first teaching point on the universality of God's power. This paragraph indicates that there are two dimensions to this power: the created universe in general and human history in particular—God is "Lord of the universe" and "master of history". These are subsidiary to the key teaching point—they are elements of further explanation that one can give if time allows. In addition, twelve references to Scripture are provided. We will be focusing on the unique place of the Scriptures in the pedagogy of God in the next chapter, but with reference to this discussion of the selection of the key teaching points we can see that the *Catechism* is pointing to the Scriptures that provide us with a wealth of material for prayer, inspiration, and further explanation.

- *The key points in the section are linked to each other.* The sections in the *Catechism* work as integrated wholes in themselves. A section is not simply a series of disconnected points, but flows in a single presentation oriented around, or culminating in, the central truths in the Faith. When we select our key teaching points, then, we also want to show how they are related to each other. Let us look at how this picture of a single, progressive presentation is developed in CCC 268–74.

CCC 269 offers us our first teaching point, on the universality of God's power. Then in CCC 270 we have the second teaching point, on the loving nature of God's omnipotence. But this is not a separate point. The fatherly nature of God characterizes the way in which we are to understand God's Lordship of creation and mastery of history. God's omnipotence is always a "fatherly omnipotence": "God is the *Father* Almighty, whose fatherhood and power shed light on one another" (CCC 270). CCC 272 continues the gradual building of the argument by introducing the third teaching point. We have seen that God's power is universal and is fatherly; now we learn that it is mysterious. And the mystery is brought out for us in a magnificent way that goes right to the heart of the Faith:

> [I]n the most *mysterious* way God the Father has revealed his almighty power in the voluntary humiliation and Resurrection of his Son, by which he conquered evil. Christ crucified is thus "the power of God and the wisdom of God" (emphasis added).[5]

We know that God's power is almighty because it has conquered evil. But how the conquering has taken place is paradoxical: it has been achieved through weakness, through humiliation. And thus we have the climax of the argument that the picture of God's almighty power we need to have is of Christ crucified. "Christ crucified is thus the 'power of God'." The presentation has drawn us inexorably into the heart of the Faith, around one of the foundational truths, the Paschal mystery. How far we seem to have moved from the opening lines speaking of the "Mighty One of Jacob". And yet none of the key teaching points have been left behind; rather, we have seen the steady development of a whole, coherent picture of the Faith.

Finally, to conclude our analysis of this section, it is worth noting how CCC 273 then presents us with a model of faith in God's almighty power in the person of our Lady. The authors are stressing that it is the beauty of the lives of believers that authenticates the Faith. This takes us back to our considerations in an earlier chapter, that one of our pedagogical keys is to select examples that reflect the life of holiness and happiness in order to provide living illustrations of the points we are making. It is the truth revealed in human lives that offers us one of the most compelling reasons for handing ourselves over more deeply into the life of Christ in the Church.

Memorization, sources, and tone

We can now notice one further aid provided for us as we select our key teaching points, and this is the "In Brief" paragraphs, which

---

[5] CCC 272, quoting 1 Cor 1:24.

conclude each section of text. For the text we have been examining we find the "In Brief" paragraphs at CCC 275–78. The introduction to the *Catechism* describes the purpose of these paragraphs as that of summing up "the essentials of that unit's teaching in condensed formulae" and suggesting "to local catechists brief summary formulae that could be memorized" (CCC 22).

It is instructive to notice that these short statements concluding each section are largely drawn from the primary sources of the Faith, especially Scripture, liturgy, the Fathers, and the creeds of the Church. They help to foster what John Paul II, in *Fidei Depositum*, described as a "catechesis renewed at the living sources of the faith". The *Catechism* here is encouraging catechists to use, as far as possible, the words, terms, phrases, and cadences of the sources of the Faith to proclaim the key teaching points. It is also inviting catechists to consider the importance of memorization. Let us examine each of these points.

The English mystic Thomas Traherne speaks intriguingly of "another education", which has a "taste and tincture", delicate and different, at which the tastes and tones of this world can only hint.[6] We know that catechesis is precisely the annunciation of just such "another education", breaking into our world like a shaft of light, because it flows from revelation.

In catechesis we are inviting those we catechize to be open to the light of revelation, this teaching which comes "from above" (Jn 3:31), we are encouraging a docility and sensitivity to the work of the Holy Spirit, who desires to deepen and make more vivid and personal that "birth from above" that was inaugurated at baptism. It is important, therefore, for us to bear in mind the importance of learning a "tone" appropriate for the annunciation of divine education, of God's pedagogy. "He who is of the earth belongs to the earth, and of the earth he speaks", but "he whom God has sent utters the words of God" (Jn 3:31, 34). Catechesis has, therefore, "the never-ending task of finding a language capable of communicating the word of God" (GDC 146). We have to learn a different way of speaking, and we can do this by immersing ourselves in the Church's own writings, and especially in the *Catechism*, so that we begin to use her own way of speaking. There

---

[6] See his work *Centuries* (Oxford: Oxford University Press, 1960).

is a graciousness, an elegance, a respectfulness, a sympathy, and a clarity about her language that reflects the saving truth she presents. The Church in her turn draws on the language of the channels that allow us access to God's revelation of himself in Christ: the Scriptures, the liturgy, and all that makes up the living Tradition of the Church. The "In Brief" paragraphs point us to these sources and this language, to words that evoke mystery and place one in the presence of the God who dwells in inaccessible light, yet at the same time have the precision that reflects the revealing of this mystery, the condescension of God, who speaks his word in the words of men.

We are also being invited to make room in our catechetical practice for memorization. The *Catechism* is an expression of Tradition, which holds the mystical memory of the Church. John Paul II specifically asked that the *Catechism* include "some basic formulas drawn from Scripture, Tradition, and the Church's magisterium" that might be easily memorized. In *Catechesis tradendae*, at the beginning of his pontificate, he had requested that the use of the memory be brought "back into use in an intelligent and even an original way in catechesis" and added: "The blossoms, if we may call them that, of faith and piety do not grow in the desert places of a memory-less catechesis." [7]

Some remain suspicious of any catechetical method that makes room for memorization. This downplaying of memorization goes hand in hand with a reaction against any form of "rote-learning". There are two main objections leveled against this form of learning. First, it is claimed that it is boring: memorization is presented as a dull, lifeless activity compared to more "imaginative" explorations of the Faith. Second, it is argued that children are often being asked to commit to memory doctrinal formulas and various facts about the Faith that they cannot understand: the implication is that memorization without a full understanding is of very limited value.

Both of these arguments are surely mistaken, however. There is a stage at which children love to memorize long lists of facts. As they learn number patterns it is adults who tire first as a child asks over and over, "Let's count up to a hundred again!" They delight in chanting endless rhymes, and the longer and more obscure the more to a child's liking. As G. K. Chesterton put it, "Because children have

---

[7] CT 55.

unbounding vitality, because they are in spirit fierce and free, therefore they want things repeated and unchanged. They always say, 'Do
it again'".[8] It is in fact precisely by learning the mysterious formulas
of the Church that children are introduced into a world of faith
large enough to cater to their spirit of exploration. The very lack of
understanding is an important aspect of the appeal the formulas make
to the child.

The *Catechism* also points us in the direction of that "originality" of
which John Paul II spoke, by offering us the example of our Lady. St.
Luke says of her, "Mary kept all these things, pondering them in her
heart" (2:19). We might say that Mary, in fact, is the model disciple
precisely because she "learned things by heart". The *Catechism* refers
us to this verse from Luke in two places: in the section on growth in
understanding the Faith (see CCC 94), where Mary's memorizing by
heart and consequent contemplation of the mysteries of the Faith in
her heart is a model for "the understanding of both the realities and
the words of the heritage of faith" to "grow in the life of the Church"
(CCC 94); and in the section on the prayer of Jesus, which suggests
that Mary's treasuring of the mysteries of God in her heart is the
means by which Jesus learns to pray in "his human heart" (CCC 2599).

Mary is the living memory of the Church. Her memories go back
to the dawn of salvation, to her Immaculate Conception; and, assumed
into heaven, she shares in the eternal destiny to which the whole Church
is called. In her own self our Lady embraces the beginning and end of
salvation and contains within herself the whole of the Church's Faith.
For nine months she carried the Son of God under her heart. Now
she ponders in that same heart the eternal revelation and glory that he
brought.

Identifying teaching points for *meaning*

We have looked at one aspect of selecting from the "essential doctrines" in the *Catechism* for our teaching. We can turn now to an
equally important area: identifying the meaning of the topic we are
teaching. We saw from the example of the hospital how important it

[8] G. K. Chesterton, *Orthodoxy* (1908; San Francisco: Ignatius Press, 1995), p. 65.

is to be able to state the purpose, or significance, of any topic. We need to identify the "why" of doctrine as well as the "what".

Clarifying the significance and "point" of our catechesis at the beginning of a session is akin to letting passengers in a car know the destination of a journey they are beginning. Once they know the end they can see the point of the route they are following, and the landmarks they pass make sense as part of the pattern of the journey. Mystery tours are popular and fun, but if one would like one's "catechetical journey" to be a matter of growing comprehension then it is important to explain the purpose clearly at the beginning.

We have spoken about the fact that catechesis is always "another education", inviting a different perspective. Only when this other perspective is gained will our key teaching points really begin to make sense.

An example may help us to appreciate this point. When Christopher Columbus proposed his plan to explore a trade route to the Far East, a route that would replace the treacherous, several-years' journey around Africa, he faced many critical issues. Such a journey, though potentially quite profitable, would be very costly. He faced a large financial outlay and would require royal backing for this undertaking. There was also the issue of navigation. He would be embarking upon uncharted waters, and though his ships represented the most advanced sailing and navigational technology of the time, they still depended on the often fickle winds for propulsion and direction. Logistical factors were also critical for Columbus. Because the journey had not been made before, he could only guess at the time it would take to reach his destination. He could not depend upon friendly ports along the way to replenish his supplies. He would have to carry what he needed and find a crew brave enough to join him on this daring adventure. Columbus faced issues of finance, navigation, and logistics.

However, before Columbus confronted any of these issues he first had to convince his consultants that he would not sail off the end of the world if he charted a course to the West. He had to convince them that sailing West to arrive in the Far East was a logical plan. Many did not believe that it was possible—sailing in what appeared to be the opposite direction from his destination made no sense to them. Intelligent discussion about finance, navigation, or logistics was impossible with those who did not believe the underlying truth that Columbus held, namely, that the earth was round, not flat.

Before one can catechize on a particular subject, then, one needs to establish certain fundamentals within which one's teaching will make sense. These fundamentals provide the students with the key to understanding what one is saying. Often, those one is catechizing will not be aware whether they share the "different perspective" with the catechist—it is the catechist who needs to be alert to this point and place the topic within an overall context that gives it meaning. For example, if someone were to raise the question "Why will the Church not ordain women?" underlying this question may be a number of "levels" of agreement or disagreement. Thus, does the questioner believe in God? If he believes in God, does he believe in God's self-revelation in Christ? If he assents to this, does he accept that Jesus founded the Church with a priesthood? If he accepts this, does he believe that the Church is the spouse of Christ? The questioner may have difficulties with the Church's teaching that she cannot ordain women to the priesthood at the level of not accepting the fact of revelation, or of the place of the Church within God's plan of salvation. Only by ensuring that the foundations are in place, enabling the Church's "perspective" on a doctrine to be clear, can a catechist enable those being taught to *understand* the topic. Only when Columbus explained his conviction that the earth is round was anyone able to understand his more detailed navigational plans.

The higher illuminates the lower

A helpful principle to govern our selection for *meaning*, for the *point* of the doctrine we are teaching, is that it is in the light of what is "higher" that we can understand the lower. This is a fundamental philosophical principle based on the reality of what is known as the "hierarchy of being".

The "hierarchy of being" describes the commonsense awareness that some parts of creation are more valuable than others. Because they are of a "higher order", they are more important. Therefore, one can understand the lower elements only in relation to the higher. Jesus spoke of this hierarchy when he said, "The sabbath was made for man, not man for the sabbath" (Mk 2:27); in other words, if we want to know the meaning of the Sabbath we must refer it to man and understand it in the light of the human person and his destiny. The converse is not true: we do not understand man in the light of the Sabbath, for the Sabbath is not a "high enough" reality to reveal the intelligibility of the human person.

Jesus' teaching reflects this principle again when he said, "Do not fear those who kill the body but cannot kill the soul" (Mt 10:28), and "You are of more value than many sparrows" (Mt 10:31): the soul is more important than the body and the human being than the sparrow. In general terms, the hierarchy of being expresses the truth that the animate order of creation is of higher significance than the inanimate, and the personal order than the animate.

The *Catechism* draws attention to this principle in CCC 234, a vital paragraph we have considered a number of times. Here it is declared that every element of Christian faith and life can ultimately be understood in the light of the Holy Trinity. The Holy Trinity illuminates our understanding of all other truths that we will be teaching. To present any aspect of Christian faith or life without regard to the Holy Trinity is to catechize in the dark, to leave our hearers in the dark, without the light thrown by this central mystery of faith.

The *Catechism* speaks of this principle again when it reminds us, "The revelation of divine love in Christ manifested at the same time the extent of evil and the superabundance of grace" (CCC 385; cf. Rom 5:20). Love sheds light on the darkness of evil. It is love that is intelligible, not evil. Evil can shed no light. As the New Testament gives witness, the evil man lives in the dark and avoids the light (see Jn 3:19–20; 1 Thess 5:4–5). Evil, in fact, as nonbeing, is supremely unintelligible in itself. This is why the *Catechism* goes on to teach, "To try to understand what sin is, one must first recognize *the profound relation of man to God*, for only in this relationship is the evil of sin unmasked in its true identity" (CCC 386). In the light of our true destiny we can understand what it would be to follow the path to ruin and disaster. But without the guiding light of our heavenly calling and relationship with God, all choices of paths would appear inconsequential. None would be seen as leading to glory, perhaps; and none would be seen as leading to alienation from God and from our happiness with him.

The importance of beginning with an understanding of the high truths of our nature is reinforced by the *Catechism* at the beginning of part 3, which deals with life in Christ:

"Christian, recognize your dignity and, now that you share in God's own nature, do not return to your former base condition by sinning. Remember who is your head and of whose body you are a member. Never forget that you have been rescued from the power of darkness and brought into the light of the Kingdom of God." [9]

"Recognize ... Remember ... Never forget!" These calls of St. Leo the Great from his Christmas homily in the fourth century are cited to open the *Catechism's* third part. They remind catechists only to speak of human fallenness in the light of human dignity. Catechists must not forget to speak about the terrible realities of sin and darkness in the light of the power of redemption. At the beginning of the first section of the third part, the *Catechism* refers us to this quotation from *Gaudium et Spes*, "Christ ... in the very revelation of the mystery of the Father and of his love, makes man fully manifest to himself and brings to light his exalted vocation." [10] Christ is the true face of every man. We understand ourselves and our end only in the light of Christ.

We have some clear directions, then, deriving from this principle:

- We teach all the mysteries of faith and life in the light of the Holy Trinity.

- We teach sin and evil in the light of redemption.

- We catechize on the human person in the light of man redeemed in Christ.

We allow these truths—of the Holy Trinity; of the plan and execution of the divine will in Christ; of the work of redemption achieved by Christ and communicated through his Church; and of the glory of man, made and redeemed in the image of God—to provide us with the basic purpose, significance, and perspective in which to place the selections we make.

It is important to realize that the *Catechism* offers us, not only a compendium of the Church's Faith, but also a constant sense of the intrinsic reasonableness of that Faith by providing us both with *what* the Church teaches and also *why* she teaches what she does. The authors want us to appreciate the reasonable nature of the Faith so that assent

[9] CCC 1691, citing St. Leo the Great, *Sermo 21 in nat. Dom.*, 3; PL 54:192C.
[10] GS 22, as cited in CCC 1701.

to the Church's teaching can be an act of growth in *understanding* as well as growth in faith. Faith and reason, as John Paul II stressed in his opening paragraph of the encyclical *Fides et Ratio*, are like "two wings on which the human spirit rises to the contemplation of truth".

We can confirm this point by returning to the section of the *Catechism* we examined earlier, CCC 268–74. As we read through these paragraphs we can note that *reasons are given for each of the key teaching points*. In the introductory paragraph, CCC 268, we can note that after each italicized item there is a comma and the word "for". In other words, we are being told the reason in summary form for each of the key teaching points. Thus: "We believe that his might is *universal*, for God who created everything also rules everything and can do everything" (CCC 268). In other words, the universality of God's might follows from the fact that he is the creator and sustainer of all that exists. Again, "God's power is *loving*, for he is our Father." The *Catechism* is telling us that the Fatherhood of God is the context for understanding God's loving nature. We can read through the paragraphs in detail, identifying for ourselves what we can call the "reason" words in the section, words such as "because", "therefore", "for", and "since". These are showing us where reasons are being adduced for the Church's teaching.

When we examine these reasons that are offered we can see that they are pointing us toward those foundational personal realities about which we spoke in chapter 3. *It is these personal realities, in fact, that provide the perspective we need on all of the topics that we teach.*

Initial proclamation, new evangelization, and conversion

What we have discovered so far can provide us with a further insight into the work of catechesis: that at the very heart of our teaching *we are selecting for conversion*. Catechesis has as its goal the deepening conversion of those who receive it (see CT 20). In and through our catechesis—to whatever group and in whatever context—we are supporting the work of evangelization. The *Catechism* has been written to assist us in our participation in the outpouring of God's grace for this fundamental task.

In its ongoing reflections upon this aim of catechesis, the Magisterium has identified three stages in the overall process of conversion, or "evangelization" (see GDC 60–72). These are sometimes referred to as the three "moments" of evangelization. The first is that of *initial*, or *"primary"*, *proclamation of the gospel*. John Paul II described this as being, in its simplest form, the good news about being "loved and saved by God" (RM 44). Or we might think of the way in which this initial proclamation is expressed in the well-known texts of John 3:16 or 2 Corinthians 5:19. This basic proclamation of the gospel is what enables a person to make an initial act of faith—it is in response to this that the first moment of conversion can occur.

The second "moment" or "stage" is that of *baptismal catechesis*—the comprehensive, systematic, and organic presentation of the Faith with which the *Catechism* is concerned. Here is the "principal place" of conversion in which one "renounces evil and gains salvation" (CCC 1427), handing oneself over to "the standard of teaching" (Rom 6:17) and into the death of Christ for "the forgiveness of all sins and the gift of new life" (CCC 1427).

The third moment is described as "on-going", or *continuing education in the Faith*. God is infinite and his plan of grace rich beyond measure. A continuing catechesis enables the baptized person to be drawn more and more deeply into communion with Christ.

There are two points worth noticing about these three moments in evangelization. The first point is that *all three moments are concerned with the call to conversion*. The *Catechism*, in fact, speaks of conversion as an "uninterrupted task for the whole Church" (CCC 1428). Our catechesis, therefore, is always given for the sake of conversion, whether the fundamental conversion in baptism or an ongoing work of purification and renewal.

The second point is that, *although these moments appear to be sequential, this is often not the case*. A group of people who can benefit from initial proclamation are those baptized Christians who have "lost a living sense of the faith, or even no longer consider themselves members of the Church, and live a life far removed from Christ and his Gospel" (RM 33). These are people we live among; they are neighbors; we have seen them in Church in the past but now they have abandoned the Faith. John Paul II coined a technical term when speaking of the Church's mission to these people. He spoke of "a new evangelization". He meant a renewed evangelization in which a primary proclamation of God's love for them and the salvation he offers them in Jesus is made explicit. It is the case with many of these people that there is little interior grasp of the realities of the gospel and the sacraments.

What we see in the *Catechism*, then, is that the fundamentals of the Faith, enshrining initial or primary proclamation, are placed at the heart of every section, so that, in and through the transmission of catechesis, there can also be a reawakening of the call to conversion at this most fundamental level. This means that, in selecting the fundamental personal realities that lie at the heart of the Faith for one's "perspective", to provide the key "meaning" of a topic or doctrine, one will also be selecting for conversion, introducing those one catechizes to the eternal love of the Trinity.

Our understanding of these points enables us to identify two further pedagogical keys.

KEY 8 FAITHFUL

We select our key teaching points for any topic with the aid of the *Catechism*, alert to the specific needs of those we are catechizing, and fostering an ongoing learning "by heart", drawing on the language of Scripture and Tradition.

KEY 9 EVANGELIZING

We place our teaching points within the primary proclamation of the Faith, enabling a clearer understanding as well as a deepening conversion.

Chapter Seven

A Scriptural and Liturgical Pedagogy:
The Word Made Flesh

Following the request of the Extraordinary Synod of Bishops in 1985, the *Catechism* is both *scriptural* and *liturgical* in its presentation of the Faith (see *Fidei Depositum*). In asking for this, the bishops clearly intended it to be understood that not only the *Catechism*, but *the whole of the work of catechesis is scriptural and liturgical in character*. They were asking that the *Catechism* model and express this character in its pages. In the chapter that follows, then, we will examine the ways in which the *Catechism*—and therefore our own catechesis—is scriptural and liturgical.

Teaching from the Scriptures and the liturgy

The *Catechism* both offers *explicit principles* concerning the use of liturgy and Scripture in catechesis (for example, CCC 101–41, 1075, 1124), and also, more broadly, it *models* such a use on every page. The clues we need to gather follow from an attentive reading of the *Catechism* as a whole, and not only from the paragraphs particularly concerned with articulating the nature of a scriptural or liturgical catechesis.

Where do we start? Perhaps from the very beginning of the text. Beginnings are always important. The direction in which you start to walk determines your likely destination. The first words of a good speaker capture the audience's attention. Opening phrases and sentences are vital.

Scripture

It is with interest that we can recall that the Prologue of the *Catechism* opens with three scriptural quotations, quotations that sum up the whole purpose of the *Catechism*: John 17:3; 1 Timothy 2:3–4; and Acts 4:12. *Scripture leads the presentation of doctrine*. It is not a mere add-on or afterthought. Throughout the *Catechism* we see a similar use of Scripture—not a use simply to confirm or elaborate the presentation of doctrines derived from nonscriptural sources (a use of Scripture often described as "proof-texting"), but rather one in which Scripture is itself the "driving force" of doctrine, its inspired source.

The Second Vatican Council has asked that in the work of theology Scripture be seen as its "soul",[1] and that is what we find in the *Catechism*. Scripture provides the soul, or "form", in and through which the doctrine of the Faith is proclaimed and unfolded for our attention; it provides *the starting point* for the presentation of doctrine, and it provides *its heart*. It is difficult to read very far in the *Catechism* without realizing that the doctrines it contains are permeated with Sacred Scripture. The *Catechism* is heavily footnoted with references to the Scriptures from which these doctrines are drawn, and the text of the *Catechism* itself is a tapestry of scriptural phrases and allusions. Cardinal Ratzinger wrote that the *Catechism* "is shaped from one end to the other by the Bible. As far as I know, there has never been until now a catechism so thoroughly formed by the Bible."[2] What we can see, therefore, is that our own catechetical practice should be *driven by Scripture* and *immersed in Scripture*.

This means that we need to be able to answer the question, in the case of any particular topic we are teaching, "What is the specific scriptural 'driving force' behind this doctrine?" In some cases this might be fairly obvious. For example, it is difficult to teach on the Real Presence of Christ in the Eucharist without making reference to the account of the Last Supper in the synoptic Gospels (Mt 26:26–28; Mk 14:22–24; Lk 22:19–20) and the Bread of Life discourse found in the sixth chapter of St. John's Gospel ("He who eats my flesh and drinks my blood has eternal life, and I will raise him up at the last day. For my flesh is food indeed, and my blood is drink indeed"; Jn 6:54–55).

In the last resort, however, there is no simple answer to this question as to the particular driving force, since it is only the catechist familiar with his own audience who can adequately discern the most

---

[1] Decree on the Training of Priests, *Optatam Totius* 16.
[2] Joseph Ratzinger, *Gospel, Catechesis, Catechism* (San Francisco: Ignatius Press, 1997), p. 61.

appropriate passage and who is able to deliver the unchanging truth of God to that specific audience in a way most suited to its situation. So, for instance, for Catholics who are quite familiar with the discourse in John's Gospel, it may be more helpful to lead an explanation of this doctrine using some of the Scriptures that describe the Old Testament prefigurements of the Eucharist—the bread of the presence kept in the temple (Ex 25:30; Num 4:7); the manna that God provided for his people in the desert (Ex 16:15); and the bread and wine offered by Melchizedek (Gen 14:18). More important still may be the Scriptures that describe the Incarnation and thus present a direct parallel to the incarnational character of this sacrament: "And the Word became flesh and made his dwelling among us" (Jn 1:14). If the eternal God would empty himself to take on human flesh in order to reveal himself to humanity, would it not be consistent that he also provide that very flesh as a sign of his presence for all people of all times?

In most cases, then, the catechist knows his audience best, and doctrine will be delivered most effectively by those passages of Scripture that meet the audience's specific needs. Is your audience predominantly ignorant of Scripture? In this case, you might wish to use the most common references in the hope that they might recognize these and thus be able to relate better to these familiar passages. Is your audience comprised of, or influenced by, strong Bible-loving separated brethren? You may wish to use apologetic Scripture references that support Church teaching on the doctrine at hand. You may also wish to refer to less common references that may engage their curiosity and inspire them to study more. Because "*all* Scripture is inspired by God and profitable for teaching" (2 Tim 3:16; emphasis added), it is for the catechist to determine the "scriptural driving force" of each particular doctrine. The Scriptures selected will be those that are most helpful for the audience.

In order that we may determine which scriptural passages should lead our presentations and so that our explanations and expositions of the Church's Faith might be soaked in Scripture, it is important that we ourselves, as catechists, have a familiarity with Sacred Scripture that is relatively uncommon among Catholics today. And yet, this is not a new requirement for catechists. The Fathers of the Second Vatican Council reaffirmed what had always been necessary for teachers of the Faith when they taught: "Therefore, all clerics ... and others

who, as deacons or catechists, are officially engaged in the ministry of
the Word, should immerse themselves in the Scriptures by constant
reading and diligent study."[3] Frank Sheed, the founder of the Catholic Evidence Guild in London, exhorts us in a similar fashion:

> The teacher of Religion should be absolutely soaked in the New Tes-
> tament, so that she knows what every key chapter in it is about; knows
> the line of thought of every book of it, could find her way about it
> blindfolded. That seems to me an indispensable minimum.[4]

Words like "immersed" and "soaked" imply more than just a passing
familiarity; "constant reading and diligent study" imply a serious, daily
activity. These appeals from the Church to her catechists are neither
unrealistic nor far-fetched when one takes seriously the fact that Scripture really does provide the "soul" of catechesis.

The more one becomes immersed in Scripture, then, the easier it is
to determine the scriptural basis of any doctrine. The most indispensable tool for this task is the *Catechism of the Catholic Church*. It is always
a good idea to find in the *Catechism* the topic you are going to teach
and take note of the scriptural footnotes in that section. It can then
become a "catechetical habit" always to prepare a presentation by first
of all reading all of the scriptural references in the *Catechism* on the
particular topic at hand. The cross-references in the *Catechism*'s mar-
gins can also be consulted for further scriptural references that may be
contained in related topics. Because Scripture is the soul of doctrine
the preparation for teaching will always seem very much like Bible
study.[5] Other important scriptural tools for preparing to teach are an
approved Catholic version of the Scriptures and a concordance.[6]

---

[3] DV 25. In fact, this exhortation is aimed at all of the faithful: "The sacred Synod
forcefully and specifically exhorts all the Christian faithful ... to learn 'the surpassing knowledge of Jesus Christ' (Phil. 3:8) by frequent reading of the divine Scriptures" (DV 25).

[4] Frank Sheed, *Are We Really Teaching Religion?* (London: Sheed and Ward, 1953), p. 9.

[5] "Proof-texting" is not completely antithetical to the method we are suggesting, but
rather represents a certain misplaced set of priorities regarding divine revelation. Scripture
drives doctrine; it is not "added on" as a supplement. By beginning the study and delivery
of doctrine with Scripture, our understanding and that of our hearers will come from the
very source of the doctrine.

[6] The *Catechism of the Catholic Church* references the Revised Standard Version. Whichever version you choose, it is helpful to have a concordance corresponding to that translation. A concordance is an alphabetical compilation of words found within Scripture. For
each word it lists the verses in which that word is found in Scripture, and it often includes

Let us sum up what we have discovered so far. It appears to be evident that, as catechists, we need to make the reading and study of Scripture a part of our daily lives. In doing so we will be giving God the best opportunity we can for him to help us in our teaching. We need to soak ourselves thoroughly in Scripture. Then, when preparing to teach, we have seen that we need to find our topic in the *Catechism of the Catholic Church* and read the Scripture references contained in the footnotes. Then we can use the cross-references in our Bible, or find related Scripture passages using a concordance, until we can recognize the full force of Scripture's driving influence on the doctrine at hand. For the session itself if we start with Scripture we will avoid the tendency to "proof-text"—that is, to add Scripture passages only after we have prepared our presentation. We have also seen that, as we prepare, we need to evaluate our audience, as well as our understanding of the doctrine so that we can select the Scripture passages that will most effectively deliver doctrine to our particular audience.

Liturgy

The presentation of doctrine in the *Catechism* is scriptural; it is also liturgical. The Church has expressed the unity between liturgy and doctrine through the ancient formula *lex orandi, lex credendi*—the rule of prayer is the rule of faith (see CCC 1124). Pope Pius XII wrote in *Mediator Dei* in 1947 that "whenever there was a question of defining a truth revealed by God, the Sovereign Pontiff and the Councils in their recourse to the 'theological sources', as they are called, have not seldom drawn many an argument from this sacred science of the liturgy" (no. 48).

In fact, this formula follows the Scriptures closely, especially 1 Timothy 2:1–4, the final verses of which, as we saw, are cited at the opening of

---

a short phrase to show the context in which the word is found. The concordance is especially useful if one's Bible is not extensively cross-referenced, because it allows us to quickly find passages that are related to the verses we are studying. For example, when studying a topic in the New Testament, the concordance will help us find where the same topic is covered in the Old Testament. It is also very helpful for finding verses that one remembers having read or heard before, but is unable to locate. Almost all of the computer versions of the Bible have a word-search function that essentially serves the same purpose as the concordance. There are many other tools that may be helpful in one's Scripture study. Often these resources can be found in the library. They include Bible dictionaries, biblical atlases, commentaries, and etymological resources that trace the origins of words.

the *Catechism* to provide us with our fundamental orientation. At the beginning of chapter 2 the Apostle Paul urges that first of all "supplications, prayers, intercessions and thanksgivings" be made for all men, supplications and prayers that grace may be poured out in order for "all men to be saved", and then "to come to the knowledge of the truth". In and through the *lex orandi* or *lex supplicandi*, one learns the Faith of the Church, and the virtue of faith—that inner light by which we perceive the truths of the Faith—is deepened and fostered. Aidan Kavanagh offers us for consideration the example of the life of St. Augustine in this respect:

> Throughout Augustine's own life as a rather wandering catechumen for thirty years, he had been deeply enfolded by the Church's *legem supplicandi*. As he himself tells, the sound of Christians singing and the thunder of the Amens rolling through the basilicas in which they worshipped moved him farther toward faith than did his own sharp-edged arguments against the Manichees. In fact, the Church's *legem supplicandi* was during this whole time constituting a *lex credendi* in Augustine's life which became finally irresistible. . . . The Church's discipline of worship did not produce Augustine's faith, but it does seem to have prodded its emergence, given it its foundation in the real order of the time, and shaped it to the point that it became recognizable to Augustine himself and accessible to others.[7]

The liturgy expresses *what* we believe.[8] At the same time, as this passage about St. Augustine suggests, through the efficacy of the sacramental liturgy, which provides us with the life of grace, *faith*[9] is established and then deepened in our lives.

If we look first of all at the role of the liturgy in establishing the *fides quae*, the Faith of the Church, we can note that it is for this reason that we find that liturgical texts are a key source in the *Catechism* used to present the Faith. It is instructive to use the index of liturgical citations in the *Catechism* in order to see how the *Catechism*

---

[7] Aidan Kavanagh, *On Liturgical Theology* (New York: Pueblo Publishing, 1984), pp. 98–99.

[8] *Fides quae*, meaning faith in the sense of that which we believe, that which is given in revelation. We find some of the earliest appeals to liturgical texts as a sure guide for determining the Faith of the Church in the work of St. Basil the Great (d. A.D. 379), for example, in his *On the Holy Spirit*.

[9] *Fides qua*, the first of the theological virtues, a virtue that is possible only because of God's work in the soul.

employs these texts. For example, Eucharistic texts appear in all four pillars of the *Catechism*, while the Rites of specific sacraments are intrinsic to the unfolding of each of them. Liturgies of both East and West are cited in order to give expression to the importance of drawing from both "lungs" of Tradition in this vital matter. The Preface of Christmas I from the Roman Missal—that in Jesus "we recognize in him God made visible, [so that] we may be caught up through him in the love of things invisible." (CCC 477)—is cited in defense of the Church's teaching that the Word assumed a true human body, and that images of this body may be venerated. The Preface of Christ the King is used as the culminating reference in the exposition of section 1 of "Life in Christ", highlighting the proclamation of the kingdom as the center of the Lord's teaching, and focusing Christian energies on living with the mind of Christ in order to *"hasten the coming of the Reign of God"* (CCC 2046).

These examples illustrate the way in which there is a liturgical, as well as a scriptural, "character" to the whole of the *Catechism*. Thus, to take one further example, in the section on the names and titles of Jesus[10] there are four related parts, examining "Jesus" (CCC 430–35), "Christ" (CCC 436–40), "The Only Son of God" (CCC 441–45), and "Lord" (CCC 446–51). In each case, the treatments are "driven" by a scriptural understanding, with biblical references as the overwhelmingly significant source. The section reaches its climax with a reference to prayer and liturgy, so that doctrine is seen clearly to lead one to the liturgy and the saving work of God (CCC 451). Again, while contemplating the meaning of the name "Jesus", the *Catechism* says, "The name of Jesus is at the heart of all Christian prayer. All liturgical prayers conclude with the words 'through our Lord Jesus Christ'."[11]

Catechesis for "the mystery"

We have seen, then, that the *Catechism* has a scriptural and liturgical character, and that this can provide a model for us in our own work. We have not yet begun to explore the exciting depths of this fact, nor

---

[10] This is a section that Cardinal Ratzinger described as "among the richest and most profound texts of the Catechism", quietly incorporating "the truly solid results of modern exegesis" (Ratzinger, *Gospel, Catechesis, Catechism*, p. 65).

[11] CCC 435.

why the liturgy provides us with far more than a set of texts from which to teach, but is in fact "the privileged place for catechizing the People of God" (CCC 1074). This latter point arises from the fact that the sacramental liturgy is the place, above all, for encountering the mystery of Christ and for receiving and participating in the life of grace. Liturgy is the place of encounter, of grace, and of conversion. This is why we are asked to catechize both *toward the liturgy* and also *from the liturgy*.

To approach the center of the Church's reasoning on this point we might return briefly to the Emmaus narrative, which we examined in chapter 5. The *Catechism* describes the Risen Lord as providing us here with his "Paschal catechesis" (CCC 1094). The Risen Christ is catechizing his downcast disciples about the reality and mode of his presence in what the *Catechism* calls the "new era". In this "age of the Church Christ now lives and acts in and with his Church, in a new way appropriate to this new age" (CCC 1076). As the followers of Christ journey "on the Way" after the Spirit has revealed this new era, and until the Lord comes again in glory, their hearts will be ablaze with the Spirit as they participate in the outpouring and "dispensing" of grace in the celebration of the Church's sacramental liturgy. We see here the role of catechesis in preparation for the liturgy.

When the two disciples on their way to Emmaus encountered Jesus, their "eyes were kept from recognizing him" until he "took the bread and blessed and broke it", even though he had explained the Scriptures to them earlier "they said to each other," 'Did not our hearts burn within us?'" as they listened (Lk 24:13–35). This "meeting" provides us with an excellent example of the primacy of the liturgy in catechetical pedagogy. The *sacramental encounter* with Christ in the Eucharist is the purpose for which the explanation of the Scriptures had prepared his disciples; and no amount of further instruction could accomplish what one liturgical event did!

The Emmaus story is also helpful in understanding the importance of the Eucharist itself. Instead of staying awhile with them, as requested by his disciples, Jesus made it clear that his incarnate presence, in which all were to recognize him now, would be under the appearances of bread and wine "until he comes again". This event was an "epiphany" of the Lord for it was a manifestation of the manner in which he would remain with his followers (see Mt 28:20). Catechetically, it provides a most useful illustration of the importance that Jesus placed on his *sacramental presence* in the Eucharist even while he was still on earth.

Finally, the Emmaus event indicates the centrality of the Eucharist in this era of salvation history. Strengthened and eager after their "liturgical" encounter, the two disciples changed course and returned to their still doubting brethren in Jerusalem to witness to the truth of the Resurrection. The Eucharist henceforth would prove to be "way-bread" for Jesus' followers, the *sacramental source* of all that is necessary to live his life and to preach his gospel. The Eucharistic table would provide his presence, an encounter with him and sustenance beyond man's wildest dreams!

The phrase that the *Catechism* uses to describe this liturgical event is the "dispensation of the mystery" (CCC 1076). The title given to the second part of the *Catechism* is, in fact, "The Celebration of the Christian Mystery". It is within this dispensing and celebrating in the sacramental liturgy of the mystery that the Scriptures also find their place, as the Emmaus narrative indicates. The key concept that we need to understand as fully as possible, therefore, for the sake of our catechesis, is that of "the mystery". The *Catechism* invites us to begin from an understanding of the "mystery" of God in his trinitarian glory and the Holy Trinity's plan for our salvation, and from there to come to an appreciation of how we are more and more deeply inserted into this mystery *in and through a scriptural and liturgical catechesis.*

Mystery and sacrament

The rediscovery of the biblical and patristic vision of the "mystery" is a major contribution of the Second Vatican Council. This rediscovery was made possible by a number of important theological studies, many of which took care to indicate the catechetical consequences of this renewal.[12] The *Catechism* incorporates the valuable results of this research. Let us read the main texts concerning "mystery" and "sacrament".

First, the mystery refers to God himself, who "transcends all creatures" as well as our language and understanding: "Our human words

[12] There are studies, for example, by Mattias Joseph Scheeben, Karl Rahner, Henri de Lubac, Yves Congar, and G. Gustav Martelet. On this historical background to the rediscovery of "the mystery", see Yves Congar, *A Messianic People* (Paris: Cerf, 1975).

always fall short of the mystery of God" (CCC 42). In the second place, "mystery" also refers to God's saving plan. In fact, the *Catechism* teaches that when he reveals his mysterious name in the burning bush (Ex 3:14), God reveals both that "he is the 'hidden God', his name is ineffable" and also that "he is the God who makes himself close to men" (CCC 206; cf. Is 45:15; Judg 13:18). Therefore, God's mystery is not so much an obscure reality as his "fascinating and mysterious presence" (CCC 208), his holiness and his faithfulness, before which man has to acknowledge his littleness and his need for forgiveness.

It is also in this light that we speak of the "mystery of the Most Holy Trinity"—not as an incomprehensible enigma but as a dazzling reality, "the source of all the other mysteries of faith, the light that enlightens them" (CCC 234). That is why we have to open our minds to this excess of light, putting away false images, so that we can "enter into his mystery as he is and as the Son has revealed him to us" (CCC 2779).

In the light of these introductory remarks we can now turn to the extraordinarily rich paragraph that opens the second part of the *Catechism*:

> In the Symbol of the faith the Church confesses *the mystery of the Holy Trinity* and of the plan of God's "good pleasure" for all creation: the Father accomplishes *the "mystery of his will"* by giving his beloved Son and his Holy Spirit for the salvation of the world and for the glory of his name (Eph 1:9). Such is *the mystery of Christ*, revealed and fulfilled in history according to the wisely ordered plan that St. Paul calls the *"plan of the mystery"* and the patristic tradition will call the "economy of the Word incarnate" or the "economy of salvation." [13]

Clearly the notion of "the mystery" lies at the very heart of the *Catechism*'s understanding of the liturgy and the sacraments. In this paragraph the mystery refers first of all to the triune God and what he does for us in his wise plan of salvation. The paragraph also helps us to see why we speak of the Paschal *mystery*, which is the accomplishment of God's "plan of the mystery". Quoting the Second Vatican Council, [14] the *Catechism* goes on to note that it is "from the side of

---

[13] CCC 1066; our emphasis. This important passage refers to the Letter to the Ephesians (1:3–14; 3:1–13). Other Pauline texts which allude to the mystery are Rom 16:25; 1 Cor 2:7, and Col 1:26–27.

[14] Vatican Council II, The Constitution on the Liturgy, *Sacrosanctum concilium* (December 4, 1963), no. 5.

Christ as he slept the sleep of death upon the cross that there came forth 'the wondrous sacrament of the whole Church'" (CCC 1067). And it also emphasizes that we have here the source of our mission and of our daily Christian lives: "It is this mystery of Christ that the Church proclaims and celebrates in her liturgy so that the faithful may live from it and bear witness to it in the world" (CCC 1068).

Thus we can see how in the three paragraphs that open the second part of the *Catechism*, the word "mystery" is used to draw together the chief doctrines of the Faith, as well as the unity between faith and life, establishing the center of that organic unity we have seen to be so important in the *Catechism*. The paragraphs that follow (1076–1112) go on to explain in detail this "dispensation of the mystery". The sacraments are thus beautifully situated in relation to the depths of the triune God and his benevolent plan, a plan developed in the Old Covenant, fully accomplished by the Passion-Resurrection of Christ and the gift of the Spirit at Pentecost, and now present through "the wondrous sacrament of the whole Church" for the salvation of the world.

We catechize *toward the liturgy* in order to lead people to this place of encounter with the mystery, now present in and through the sacraments. History, as the arena within which the mystery of God's plan is realized, has its center in the revelation of that mystery in Christ, and catechesis points the faithful toward that center. Because Christ is eternally present to all times in and through his Resurrection and Ascension, we can say that time is a matter of "describing new circles around a sun which is radiating light and warmth. This sun is Christ and His work."[15] This "circling" around the sun takes place for the Church in the liturgical year, which therefore provides the structure for our catechetical work (see CCC 1074). The liturgical year is "Christ Himself, living on in His Church" in which the mysteries of Christ's life are "still now consistently present and active" and are "sources of divine grace for us".[16] Reflecting upon the whole scope of history, Vagaggini puts it this way:

The time before Christ ... (was) a preparation for Christ the Redeemer, Mediator, Priest, gloriously reigning Lord, and, as it were, a series of

---

[15] Joseph-Andre Jungmann, S.J., "Liturgy and the History of Salvation", *Lumen Vitae* 10 (1955): 263.

[16] Pope Pius XII, *Mediator Dei* (London: Catholic Truth Society, 1947), 176.

sketches of the reality which is completed in Christ. . . . [T]he time after Christ . . . (was) to bring about in creatures who appear on the world's stage until the end of time, the participation and assimilation of those realities of divine life which exist in the dead and risen Christ and which Christ communicates to them. . . . [I]n a very special way His resurrection marks the beginning of the last times, the *eschata*, precisely because in Christ the meaning of time and of history is realized fully.[17]

In the *Catechism*, then, the sacraments are presented in the light of Christ, the revelation of the mystery. In an important passage the *Catechism*, after having reminded us that the Greek word *mysterion* has been translated in Latin both by *mysterium* and by *sacramentum*, underlines how sacramentality is rooted in the mystery of Christ:

> In later usage the term *sacramentum* emphasizes the visible sign of the hidden reality of salvation which was indicated by the term *mysterium*. In this sense, Christ himself is the mystery of salvation: "For there is no other mystery of God, except Christ." The saving work of his holy and sanctifying humanity is the sacrament of salvation, which is revealed and active in the Church's sacraments (which the Eastern Churches also call "the holy mysteries"). The seven sacraments are the signs and instruments by which the Holy Spirit spreads the grace of Christ the head throughout the Church which is his Body.[18]

This means that in our catechesis we can approach the mystery by way of the sacraments, for in this way we can enable those whom we teach to deepen their understanding of, and participation in, the mystery: "Liturgical catechesis aims to initiate people into the mystery of Christ . . . by proceeding from the visible to the invisible, from the sign to the thing signified, from the 'sacraments' to the 'mysteries'."[19]

As catechists we aim to "initiate people into the mystery of Christ". And the *Catechism* teaches us that *Christ is both mystery and sacrament*. He is *the mystery*, since he sums up in himself the whole design of God. He is also *sacrament* since

> everything in Jesus' life was a sign of his mystery (cf. Lk 2:7; Mt 27:48; Jn 20:7). His deeds, miracles, and words all revealed that "in him the

---

[17] Cyprian Vagaggini, O.S.B., *Theological Dimensions of the Liturgy* (London: Geoffrey Chapman, 1985), p. 15.
[18] CCC 774, citing St. Augustine, *Epistulae* 187, 11, 34; PL 33:846.
[19] CCC 1075.

whole fullness of deity dwells bodily" (Col 2:9). His humanity appeared as "sacrament," that is, the sign and instrument, of his divinity and of the salvation he brings: what was visible in his earthly life leads to the invisible mystery of his divine sonship and redemptive mission.[20]

The whole of our liturgical catechesis, therefore, moving from the seen to the unseen and from the sacrament to the mystery, takes place "in Christ". During his earthly life Jesus brought about our salvation through signs, words, and deeds (see CCC 1115); now the sacraments are "efficacious signs of grace", "visible rites" by that "divine life is dispensed to us" (CCC 1131). The sacraments use signs and symbols that are adapted to us as bodily-spiritual wholes (see CCC 1145–52). They are both words and deeds (see CCC 1084, 1153–55).

The importance given to sacrament and mystery in the *Catechism* enables us to appreciate several vital points:

- that the whole of God's plan is sacramental and we can speak of a "sacramental structure" to the pedagogy of God.[21] Catechesis takes place inside this context. Our catechesis has a *sacramental structure*.

- that the goal of catechesis is *to enable a participation in God's life, both now on earth and for eternity in heaven*. Catechesis is to lead to a life "in the mystery"—a life that is "mystical" in the original sense—"because it participates in the mystery of Christ through the sacraments—'the holy mysteries'—and, in him, in the mystery of the Holy Trinity" (CCC 2014).

- that *catechesis is necessarily ecclesial*: it comes from the Church and it is for the Church. The sacraments are "by the Church" and "for the Church" (CCC 1118), the Church being a priestly community united to Christ by her ordained ministers (see CCC 1121, 1132, 1140–44), and living together from the same

---

[20] CCC 515.

[21] In fact, the *Catechism* uses the words of the Dogmatic Constitution on Divine Revelation of Vatican II (*Dei Verbum*) to set out the "divine pedagogy" of the revelation that God makes of his own mystery: "The divine plan of Revelation is realized simultaneously 'by deeds and words which are intrinsically bound up with each other'" (CCC 53 citing DV 2). These expressions, used in DV 2 to describe the economy of revelation, clearly refer to sacramentality.

Paschal mystery in the diversity of catholicity (see CCC 1200–1206). This point helps us to understand the deep connection that exits between teaching the Faith and celebrating the mystery of Christ in the liturgy of the Church.

A unity: The Word becomes flesh

The work of catechesis draws its life from the mystery and is oriented toward the mystery: by emphasizing this, the *Catechism* helps us to see the vital importance of *holding Scripture and liturgy together*, as an ongoing epiphany of the Risen Lord as the Word Made Flesh. As we noted at the beginning of this chapter, the whole of the *Catechism* has a scriptural and liturgical character. We now see that they form a unity. The Word and the Spirit, as the two "hands" of the Father, carry out their "joint mission" of love (see CCC 702–4), and the Scriptures and the liturgy are the living media of this mission. Holding together Scripture and liturgy reflects the fact that God's pedagogy has its climax in an embodiment. The Holy Spirit overshadows the Virgin to enable the conception of the Word in the womb of Mary (see Lk 1:35). "The Word became flesh and dwelt among us, full of grace and truth" (Jn 1:14). And it is from this embodiment, found in the dispensation of the mystery in the sacramental liturgy, at the tables of the Word and the Eucharist, that the faithful are enabled to contemplate and be drawn into the very heart of the mystery, in and through Christ.

The Orkney poet Edwin Muir wrote movingly of the desolation caused by a form of scriptural Christianity removed from the living, enfleshed presence of the Lord:

> The windless northern surge, the sea-gull's scream,
> And Calvin's kirk crowning the barren brae ...
> How could our race betray
> The Image, and the Incarnate One unmake
> Who chose this form and fashion for our sake?
>
> The Word made flesh is here made word again,
> A word made word in flourish and arrogant crook ...
> And there the logical hook

On which the Mystery is impaled and bent
Into an ideological instrument . . .

The fleshless word, growing, will bring us down,
Pagan and Christian man alike will fall . . .
Invisibly will fall:
Abstract calamity, save for those who can
Build their cold empire on the abstract man.[22]

The living Word worshipped by Christians is an enfleshed Word. Far from separating us from the realm of spirit, this enfleshing is the route by which we gain access to the transcendent. And through the economy of salvation "the spiritual beauty of God", made visible in Christ, is now "reflected in the most holy Virgin Mother of God, the angels, and saints" (CCC 2502), as well as in the liturgical signs and images by which "the mystery celebrated is imprinted in the heart's memory" (CCC 1162).

We have already met the ancient formula *lex orandi, lex credendi*, to which is often added *lex vivendi* since how we pray and believe is inseparable from how we live: thus *lex orandi, lex credendi, lex vivendi*. To this we can draw out the implicit importance of the annunciation of the Word in the liturgy: *lex orandi, lex legendi, lex credendi, lex vivendi*.

The rule of how we receive God's revelation in and through the liturgy and the Scriptures, praying and reading, is the rule by which we believe and live. The formula provides a beautiful and concise expression of the pedagogy of God. The *Catechism* constantly articulates this unity of word, worship, faith, and life so that we can appreciate how catechesis must orient itself by this. Every Sunday and every Feast Day the Church proclaims the divine Word in the context that Christ entrusted to her, the re-presentation of his saving act. The Word of God; the Church's prophetic and catechetical role in proclaiming the Word; her mandate to celebrate the Eucharist and the other sacraments; and the life of the faithful flowing from the sacred mysteries— these together form an integrated whole. Dom Theodore Ghesquiere explained it this way:

---

[22] "The Incarnate One", from Edwin Muir's *Collected Poems* (London: Faber and Faber, 1960).

The message of the divine word, borne by the Church to all human generations, becomes in the liturgy a living word, efficacious and up to date, in which the people of the messianic times discover the secret of their destiny in the light of the Holy Spirit.[23]

A short paragraph from the second part of the *Catechism* ensures that we understand that this vibrant, organic whole flows from the work of the Son and the Spirit, sent from the heart of the Father, and now made present in the Scriptures and the liturgical celebration, thus bringing us to faith and providing the inner energy for our lives:

The Holy Spirit gives a spiritual understanding of the Word of God to those who read or hear it, according to the dispositions of their hearts. By means of the words, actions, and symbols that form the structure of a celebration, the Spirit puts both the faithful and the ministers into a living relationship with Christ, the Word and Image of the Father, so that they can live out the meaning of what they hear, contemplate, and do in the celebration.[24]

The paragraph also speaks of the "spiritual understanding of the Word of God". The Church has always believed herself to be invited by the Holy Spirit to search out the spiritual depths of the Scriptures beyond the literal sense of passages, in order to discern there more and more deeply the revelation of the mystery of God and his plan of salvation. Catechesis is to help the faithful "to open themselves to this spiritual understanding of the economy of salvation as the Church's liturgy reveals it and enables us to live it" (CCC 1095).

The *Catechism* bears constant witness to this appreciation of the spiritual sense of Scripture and insists that catechesis needs to take account of this sense, as well as the fact that all scriptural exegesis is based on the literal meaning:

According to an ancient tradition, one can distinguish between two *senses* of Scripture: the literal, and the spiritual, the latter being subdivided into the allegorical, moral, and anagogical senses. . . .

[23] Dom Theodore Ghesquiere, O.S.B., "Bible-Reading and Liturgical Life", *Lumen Vitae*, 1955, p. 173.
[24] CCC 1101.

The *literal sense* is the meaning conveyed by the words of Scripture and discovered by exegesis, following the rules of sound interpretation: "All other senses of Sacred Scripture are based on the literal." [25]

For example, if you were teaching about the sacrament of baptism, using the literal sense of Scripture, one starting point could be the baptism of Jesus in the Jordan (Mt 3:13–17; Mk 1:9–11; Lk 3:21–22; Jn 1:31–34). This rich text enables one to immediately make one's annunciation of this doctrine *Christ-centered* (for it concerns Jesus' own baptism), *trinitarian* (since the baptism of Jesus is an occasion of a manifestation of the three Persons of the Trinity), focused upon the *mystery of redemption* (since Jesus' baptism looks forward to his Passion), and focused upon the immense *dignity that the human person* has in God's eyes (since Jesus, in his baptism, is choosing to identify with mankind in its sin in order to bear that sin).

To deepen and further enrich this teaching, we can then move to the *spiritual senses*. The "spiritual sense" refers to the fact that "[t]hanks to the unity of God's plan, not only the text of Scripture but also the realities and events about which it speaks can be signs" (CCC 117). Both the liturgy and the *Catechism* can be for us here potent sources of reflection as we examine the ways in which the Church has developed her "spiritual understanding of the Word of God" in relation to baptism. We shall see that the spiritual senses of Scripture assist in the formation of the theological virtues.

The first spiritual sense is the *allegorical sense*, by which we "acquire a more profound understanding of events by recognizing their significance in Christ" (CCC 117). For instance, one might move from Christ's baptism to the account of the crossing of the Red Sea (Ex 14:10–31). The literal sense of this passage is that the Israelites really were saved from the Egyptians when God held back the waters of the Red Sea. But it goes deeper than that: the crossing of the Red Sea is a sign or type of Christ's victory over death through the waters of baptism. No wonder, then, that the crossing of the Red Sea is recounted in our liturgies, especially in the blessing of the baptismal waters (see CCC 1221). By using the allegorical sense, we will reveal the never-ending love of the Father, whose providential plan progressively unfolds

[25] CCC 115–116. Paragraph 116 quotes St. Thomas Aquinas, ST 1, 1, 10 ad 1.

until it is fulfilled in Jesus Christ. Also, by recalling the cloud of witnesses who have gone before us, we will be providing examples of how others have lived in faith. "Faith is a personal act. . . . But faith is not an isolated act. . . . The believer has received faith from others and should hand it on to others" (CCC 166). *The allegorical sense speaks to faith.*

The second spiritual sense is the *moral sense,* which means that "the events reported in Scripture ought to lead us to act justly" (CCC 117). Examples of verses with a moral sense that pertain to baptism might include Jesus' washing the feet of the disciples at the Last Supper (Jn 13:1–20) or his agony in the garden (Lk 22:39–46), both of which give vivid examples of what it means to die to oneself and share in the obedience and sacrifice that are a part of the priestly and kingly anointing in baptism. Another example is Lot's wife, who failed to follow the instructions of the angel and instead looked back at the destruction of Sodom and Gomorrah, causing her to be turned into a pillar of salt (Gen 19:26). In baptism we are called to conversion: to turn toward the path of perfect love and away from sin. And yet it is still possible to gaze back at our prebaptismal life and fall into sin. *The moral sense of Sacred Scripture speaks to charity.*

The third spiritual sense of Sacred Scripture is the *anagogical* sense, by which "[w]e can view realities and events in terms of their eternal significance, leading us toward our true homeland" (CCC 117). We are seeing how Scripture points us toward a deeper appreciation and understanding of our destiny in God. For example, Noah's ark speaks of being saved from the waters of the flood, just as in baptism we receive salvation in the "ark" of the Church. Again, "the crossing of the Jordan River by which the People of God received the gift of the land promised to Abraham's descendants" is "an image of eternal life" (CCC 1222). *The anagogical sense speaks to hope,* the third of the theological virtues. The anagogical sense of Scripture shows how doctrine informs hope.

Drawing on these senses of Sacred Scripture in our catechetical sessions, then, helps us to demonstrate the links between faith and life as we show the relevance of the doctrine we are presenting to the fostering of faith, hope, and love. The liturgy is, above all, the context within which we receive the grace of the Holy Spirit, who prepares our hearts and opens our minds to enable this "spiritual understanding of the Word of God" (CCC 1101).

From this contemplation of the ways in which the *Catechism* assists us in understanding the scriptural and liturgical character of the pedagogy of God we can formulate two further keys for our catechetical work, two keys that are particularly closely united.

KEY 10 SCRIPTURAL

We let our catechesis be soaked in the Scriptures and "driven" by them, allowing the Holy Spirit to provide a spiritual understanding of the Word.

KEY 11 LITURGICAL

We teach so that those whom we are catechizing are led, in and through the liturgy, into a deeper understanding of, and participation in, the mystery.

Chapter Eight

A Prayerful Pedagogy

Prayer is the subject of the last part of the *Catechism of the Catholic Church*. Prayer is also the subject of the final chapter of this book. Inseparable from the confession of faith, the sacramental liturgy, and the moral life, prayer has its own vital and specific place within the work of catechesis. The *Catechism* demonstrates the Church's awareness of this: former catechisms gave a commentary on the Our Father, but here, for the first time in the history of the Church, we have been offered an organic presentation of Christian prayer in a document of the Magisterium (part 4, section 1). This section is perhaps the most original part of the *Catechism* and has been widely recognized as a classic text on prayer.

Prayer in the economy of the mystery

It is worthwhile pausing here to reflect for a moment on the reasons for the inclusion of the first section in the fourth part. Jean Corbon, who was the key redactor of this part of the *Catechism*,[1] points out that in the first draft of the *Catechism of the Catholic Church* there were only three parts: the Creed, on the celebration of the Christian mystery, and life in Christ. It was expected to add a brief commentary on the Lord's Prayer. But following the worldwide consultation of the episcopate and of Institutes for theology and for catechesis, there was a decision to prepare guidelines for a catechesis on Christian prayer in a fourth part, before the commentary of the Our Father.

[1] See Jean Corbon, "Maître, apprends-nous à prier: À propos de la Quatrième Partie du *Catéchisme*", in *Transmettre la Foi* (Venasque, France: Centre Notre-Dame de Vie/Editions du Carmel, 1994), pp. 165–87.

The question was raised: Is it not unwise—and even artificial—to present teaching on Christian prayer in the *Catechism* in a section distinct from the Creed, the liturgy, and from life in Christ? In the Scriptures, one cannot find a "part" dedicated to prayer: prayer is everywhere. It is true that, later, when the catechumenate began to be structured, a more didactic presentation of the apostolic catechesis appeared: the profession of baptismal faith (the Creed), teaching on the Christian life, an initiation into the mysteries (the "mystagogia"), and also the "handing over" of the Lord's Prayer. Still, even during this patristic period, there was no "general teaching" on prayer; the newly born children of God learned to pray with the prayer of the Only Son of God. Above all, they were educated to prayer as members of the ecclesial community. This last point—the ecclesial formation in prayer—is why some asked whether the section on Christian prayer in the *Catechism of the Catholic Church* might be included in the second part, placing it within the "dynamic" of the liturgy. Others asked for the teaching on prayer to be inserted at the end of the chapter on the Holy Spirit, or at the end of the third part (either within the section on life in the Spirit, or within the context of the virtue of religion).

It must be agreed that prayer cannot be a "part" of the *Catechism*, if we mean by this a part isolated from the remainder of the *Catechism*. Nevertheless, it was believed important to provide an extended teaching on prayer for our world, a world that is dying because prayer is missing and yet is searching for an authentically spiritual way of life. The *Catechism* responds to these basic needs. It does not attempt to give a complete treatise on prayer (this would need to take into account different historical and cultural contexts), nor does it seek to provide a new "program" for the development of spirituality. Rather, it gives a fundamental reference text for all the local churches, reminding us of the biblical, liturgical, anthropological, and ecclesiological foundations of prayer in the Christian life.

The authors of the *Catechism* have ensured that this section on prayer is in no way isolated from the other parts. The title of the first section is "Prayer in the Christian Life": the title is reminding us that we need to read the *Catechism* "according to the internal coherence of the Christian mystery".[2] In the *Catechism*, prayer is inseparably linked to the

---

[2] Ibid., p. 175.

other elements of the Deposit of Faith. This integration of prayer "in the Christian life" is also a response to a separation between prayer and the other aspects of the Christian life that has been disastrous for theology, for the life of the People of God, and for the work of catechesis.[3] The first paragraph of this fourth part of the *Catechism* therefore places prayer within an "organic" understanding of revelation and its transmission, summarizing the whole movement of the *Catechism* that culminates in this presentation on prayer:

> "Great is the mystery of the faith!" The Church professes this mystery in the Apostles' Creed (*Part One*) and celebrates it in the sacramental liturgy (*Part Two*), so that the life of the faithful may be conformed to Christ in the Holy Spirit to the glory of God the Father (*Part Three*). This mystery, then, requires that the faithful believe in it, that they celebrate it, and that they live from it in a vital and personal relationship with the living and true God. This relationship is prayer.[4]

The paragraph tells us that the "mystery of Christ"—which the Church professes, celebrates and lives—also needs to be personally appropriated by each believer, in a "vital and personal relationship with the living and true God". Prayer is precisely the means by which one can personally accomplish this "appropriation" of the mystery.

Before considering some of the details of this appropriation of the mystery, and its catechetical implications, let us make two preliminary remarks.

The first is that, in and through the teaching given here on prayer, we also become clearer about the role of prayer in the handing on of revelation, and also how prayer contributes to the development of the understanding of revelation in the Church. We are shown, in other

---

[3] At the beginning of the modern period, a new kind of "spiritual theology" appeared (so-called "mystical theology"), which was separated from "moral theology" (so-called "ascetical theology"). It is because of this modern separation (which we do not find in the Scriptures or in Patristic theology), that the spiritual life and prayer have almost disappeared from catechetical research. But now, after Vatican II and thanks to the work of certain theologians, this separation has been overcome; and the *Catechism of the Catholic Church* is a clear expression of this work of reunification. The chapter on "The Universal Call to Holiness in the Church" in the Second Vatican Council document *Lumen Gentium* was extremely important for challenging this thinking, and theologians who have provided invaluable work in this field include Hans Urs von Balthasar, S. Pinckaers, and F.-M. Léthel.

[4] CCC 2558.

words, *how prayer sheds light on the catechetical process*, and *how catechesis in turn sheds light on the life of prayer.*

Another important preliminary remark that we can make here is that this presentation on prayer allows us to discern what is *essential* in prayer from what is *contingent* (see CCC 11, 1205). What is provided here enables catechists to be confident that they have a normative presentation on prayer to which they can turn, part of the Deposit of Faith. The pastoral and practical consequences of this are obviously very important. Discerning what is essential can prevent catechists from becoming caught up in secondary aspects related to prayer; and it can help them to deepen their own appreciation of the essential dimensions of prayer.

Prayer as the main expression of man's relationship with God

The *Catechism* provides the essential elements of what prayer is; in CCC 2559–65 in particular we can find the Church's fundamental doctrine on prayer.

First, prayer is a cry bursting from the human heart. We are offered a definition from St. Thérèse of the Child Jesus: "For me, prayer is a surge of the heart; it is a simple look turned toward heaven, it is a cry of recognition and of love, embracing both trial and joy." [5] And the next paragraph insists on the attitude of humility that is implied in this cry: "Man is a beggar before God." [6]

This cry is also coming from God: "Paradoxically our prayer of petition is a response to the plea of the living God" (CCC 2561). Prayer is a manifestation of God's merciful and gracious love. He is searching for man. He wants to reveal and to communicate himself to man: "God thirsts that we may thirst for him" (CCC 2560).[7] So, while a human cry, prayer is always God's gift. Essentially, prayer is an encounter, "the encounter of God's thirst with ours" (ibid.).

Second, prayer is an expression of the covenant that governs the relationship between God and man. In this human act the components of the covenant appear: God's promise and gift, the human cry and answer, and consequently the communion between God and man:

[5] St. Thérèse of Lisieux, *Manuscrits autobiographiques*, C 25r.
[6] The *Catechism*, no. 2559, here is quoting St. Augustine, *Sermo* 56, 6, 9; PL 38: 381.
[7] Cf. St. Augustine, *De diversis quaestionibus octoginta tribus* 64, 4; PL 40:56.

Christian prayer is a covenant relationship between God and man in Christ. It is the action of God and of man, springing forth from both the Holy Spirit and ourselves, wholly directed to the Father, in union with the human will of the Son of God made man.[8]

Therefore, from a human point of view, prayer involves the heart, "the place of decision", "the place of truth, where we choose life or death", "the place of encounter" where "as image of God we live in relation", "the place of covenant" (CCC 2563). Essentially, prayer is a covenant relationship between God and man, and the heart is the place of this covenant.[9]

Third, prayer is communion, "the living relationship of the children of God with their Father", a life in the presence and the fellowship of the thrice-holy God, a communion of life whose "dimensions are those of Christ's love" (CCC 2565; cf. Eph 3:18–21). Far from being an egocentric introspection, Christian prayer opens one's heart to all of humanity. Essentially, prayer is a communion in Christ's love.

We can conclude, then, by saying that the essence of Christian prayer is an encounter, rooted in God's will to communicate himself to man; it is a personal and living relationship, originating in God's covenant; and it is a communion in love, God's gift and man's answer.

It is important for the catechist to distinguish between the essential reality of prayer and the forms that prayer takes. Keeping this distinction in mind prevents us from confusing the means and the end. Fr. Marie-Eugene has pointed out that prayer is *essentially* "an exchange between two loves: that which God has for us, that which we have for Him",[10] whereas its "forms" will be very different:

---

[8] CCC 2564.

[9] This polysemic word refers to a very important theme in the Scriptures and in the *Catechism* as well, especially concerning faith, the moral life, and prayer: "It is the *heart* that prays. If our heart is far from God, the words of prayer are in vain" (CCC 2562); "The heart is the place of this quest and encounter, in poverty and in faith" (CCC 2710); see also CCC 2570–71; CCC 2697 (the memory of the heart); CCC 2699–2700 (the composure of the heart); CCC 2729–33 (the heart and spiritual battle); CCC 2737–40 (the heart for petition), and so on. We can underline here that the recollection of the heart is the core of the different forms of prayer in the Christian tradition (vocal prayer, meditation, and contemplative prayer): "They have in common the recollection of the heart" (CCC 2721).

[10] Fr. Marie-Eugene of the Child Jesus, O.C.D., *I Want to See God* (New York: Resources for Christian Living, 1996), vol. 1, p. 54.

If we consider, then, the natural activities brought into play, this exchange of friendship . . . will find a new and astonishing variety in the diversity of temperaments, the differences of age and development, and even in the multiplicity of the actual dispositions of the souls who are praying.[11]

At the level of the different expressions of prayer, freedom is of the utmost importance, so that the goal—intimacy with God—can always be pursued:

Under these various forms and throughout all these vicissitudes, the exchange will remain essentially the same. Supple and active, the love that animates it will make use of means and obstacles by turn, of ardor and aridity, of intellect or imagination, external senses or pure faith. . . . Among these manifold modes and prayers, the best will be the one that will best unite the soul to God.[12]

For this clarification of the love that unites God and man in prayer, the *Catechism* invites us to consider the relationships between God and man as they take place in the history of salvation.

History of salvation, history of prayer

The covenants between God and man take place in the history of salvation. We have already seen the importance of locating doctrine within the Story of Salvation, and now the *Catechism* carefully assists us in presenting the Church's doctrine on prayer within this history. Despite man's sins and refusals, God is always looking for him, calling him to a relation, a covenant, a communion that is formed in prayer (CCC 2567). Thus, prayer is the drama of the meeting between God's grace and man's freedom, in man's heart: "As God gradually reveals himself and reveals man to himself, prayer appears as a reciprocal call, a covenant drama. Through words and actions, this drama engages the heart."[13]

Abel, Enoch, Noah, Abraham, Jacob, Moses, David and the kings, Elijah and the prophets, the psalmists—all participate in this revelation of prayer within the progressive restoration of fallen man: "Prayer is

[11] Ibid., p. 55.
[12] Ibid., pp. 55–56.
[13] CCC 2567.

bound up with human history, for it is the relationship with God in historical events" (CCC 2568).

This revelation is completed in Jesus: "The drama of prayer is fully revealed to us in the Word who became flesh and dwells among us" (CCC 2598). The catechist can find in Jesus the One who prays in him, and for him; as St. Augustine says, Jesus prays "for us", "in us", and "by us" (see CCC 2616). In Jesus, who unites in himself God and man, we see both God's thirst for us and our cry of response to him.

In terms of our response, we can say that Jesus reveals the filial character of all prayer: "His *filial* prayer, which the Father awaits from his children, is finally going to be lived out by the only Son in his humanity, with and for men" (CCC 2599). Summing up in his own prayer the cry of all humanity (see CCC 2606), therefore, Jesus teaches us how to pray. His prayer assumes different expressions (petition, intercession, thanksgiving, blessing, and so on), but in and through all of these expressions we find the "loving adherence of his human heart to the mystery of the will of the Father" (CCC 2603; cf. Eph 1:9). In the light of his trusting love, for example, Jesus shows us what asking is: "*Before* the gift is given, Jesus commits himself to the One who in giving gives himself. The Giver is more precious than the gift; he is the 'treasure'; in him abides his Son's heart; the gift is given 'as well'." [14]

Jesus teaches and expresses in his own life the unity between prayer and life (see CCC 2607), and in the Sermon on the Mount he insists on the link between the conversion of the heart and prayer. The consequence is a more faithful prayer: once committed to conversion, the heart learns to pray in faith. And faith leads to more hope (see CCC 2612) and to a deeper, more committed love (see CCC 2614). On his Cross Jesus' last words reveal that "prayer and the gift of self are but one" (CCC 2605).

As a model for us of the unity between prayer and life, the *Catechism* also presents a portrait for us of the prayer of the Virgin Mary, whose *fiat* reveals the quiet, intense beauty of prayer as a cooperation with God's plan, in faith and love: "this is Christian prayer: to be wholly God's, because he is wholly ours" (CCC 2617).

Having meditated upon prayer in the "time" of the Old Covenant and in the "fullness of time", the *Catechism* now turns to examine the

[14] CCC 2604; Mt 6:21, 33.

prayer of the apostolic Church in the fullness of the gift of the Spirit. Her forms of prayer, to which the canonical Scriptures bear witness, are part of revelation and are normative for the Church (see CCC 2625). This section is very helpful for the catechist in its identification of the different expressions of prayer: blessing, adoration, petition, intercession, and especially thanksgiving and praise, which are characteristic of the prayer of the Church, liberated by her Savior.

Baptismal life, the source of Christian prayer

The *Catechism* now brings us into the very heart of its treatment on prayer, helping us to understand that *the wellspring of prayer is Christ*, who gives us the living water of the Spirit. He provides this living water in and through

- the Word of God;

- the sacramental liturgy of the Church;

- the theological virtues: faith, hope, and charity.

We are begotten in the Christian life by the Word of God and the sacraments of the Church: the fruit of this new birth is that we are children of God, living in faith, hope, and charity, through God's grace. It is these virtues which are, in practical terms, for each of us the sources of our relationship with God.

We can understand how this is the case by referring to the effects of baptism. Quoting from the letters of St. Paul and also St. Peter, the *Catechism* summarizes them concisely: baptism makes man

> "a new creature," an adopted son of God, who has become a "partaker of the divine nature," (2 Cor 5:17; 2 Pet 1:4; cf. Gal 4:5–7), member of Christ and co-heir with him (cf. 1 Cor 6:15; 12:27; Rom 8:17), and a temple of the Holy Spirit (cf. 1 Cor 6:19).[15]

Since our baptism we are really children of God, divinized. The Spirit of the only Son cries in our hearts "Abba" (see also Gal 4:5–7; Rom 8:14–17), "God's love has been poured into our hearts through

---

[15] CCC 1265.

the Holy Spirit who has been given to us" (Rom 5:5), and we really "become partakers of the divine nature" (2 Pet 1:4).

This is so important that we need to consider it further. In the third part of the *Catechism*, the paragraphs concerning grace invite us to take these affirmations of the Scripture in a realistic sense. What is grace? It is "the gratuitous gift that God makes to us of his own life", which is "infused by the Holy Spirit into our soul"; it is this which is called "*sanctifying* or *deifying grace*"; it is "received in Baptism"; in each Christian, it is "the source of the work of sanctification".[16]

As catechists, it is important that we note the practical consequences of this reality:

> Grace is a created participation in the nature of God, in the life of God. It is not part of God. No, it is created, but it makes us children of God, it makes us like God.... This grace allows us to do works like God's works. We are not all-powerful or infinite, but it allows us to perform intellectual operations and works of love like God Himself, to enter into a relationship with Him and so to act like Him.[17]

This baptismal grace enables us to live a dynamic filial life. It gives us an orientation toward the living God and toward our own Christian perfection. The *Catechism* insists on this point:

> Grace is a *participation in the life of God*. It introduces us into the intimacy of Trinitarian life: by Baptism the Christian participates in the grace of Christ, the Head of his Body. As an "adopted son" he can henceforth call God "Father," in union with the only Son. He receives the life of the Spirit who breathes charity into him and who forms the Church.[18]

Grace *really* transforms our nature. We *really are* children of God able to live as such, in love: "Sanctifying grace is an habitual gift, a stable and supernatural disposition that perfects the soul itself to enable it to live with God, to act by his love" (CCC 2000). At the beginning of this book we emphasized the primacy of grace for catechesis—now we can see the truth of this in terms of the transformation of our lives, under the mercy of God.

[16] CCC 1999; cf. Jn 4:14; 7:38–39.
[17] Fr. Marie-Eugene, O.C.D., *Where the Spirit Breathes: Prayer and Action* (New York: Alba House, 1998), p. 36.
[18] CCC 1997.

We have already stressed that prayer is presented here as set in the midst of our Christian lives. Fr. Marie-Eugene illustrates this point by the image of a graft. Grace is grafted onto human nature, as a cutting from a hybrid rose is grafted onto the strong roots of a wild rose. Then the hybrid rose will bloom:

> What is grace on the psychological level? It is not some treasure, some jewel hidden in a corner of our soul.... No! This grace is set in our human nature. Man, the sum of creation, is material; he lives a sensory life as well as an intellectual life. This grace is engrafted onto the life of our soul; it is meant to complete, in a sense, our psychological being, to fix itself within our psychological being. Grace itself is in the essence of the soul.... It is another nature which comes to complete our purely natural nature. It is added over and above, and makes us children of God, God by participation.[19]

It is important, as we feel the growing secularization of society that, both for ourselves and for those whom we catechize, we make what we can call "an inventory of our spiritual powers".[20] The *Catechism* presents us with an uplifting statement of such an inventory in its introduction to the third part, "Life in Christ", which it summarizes in St. Paul's words, "For to me to live is Christ" (Phil 1:21). It cites St. John Eudes, who exhorts us in the following way:

> I ask you to consider that our Lord Jesus Christ is your true head, and that you are one of his members. He belongs to you as the head belongs to its members; all that is his is yours: his spirit, his heart, his body and soul, and all his faculties. You must make use of all these as of your own, to serve, praise, love, and glorify God. You belong to him, as members belong to their head. And so he longs for you to use all that is in you, as if it were his own, for the service and glory of the Father.[21]

Then again, in the second part the *Catechism* details the effects of baptismal grace in us, effects that mean that "the whole organism of the Christian's supernatural life has its roots in Baptism" (CCC 1266). Let us consider this "organism of the Christian's supernatural life". Our being is divinized by grace, as we have seen above. Our faculties

---

[19] Fr. Marie-Eugene, *Where the Spirit Breathes*, pp. 40–41.
[20] "Anxiety and disturbance must lead us to a deeper, stronger confidence in the spiritual powers which have been given to us", ibid., p. 33.
[21] CCC 1698, citing St. John Eudes, *Tract. de admirabili corde Jesu*, 1, 5.

and actions are raised as well: grace allows us to act as children of God, with our corporal members, our senses, and our faculties of knowledge and will. In heaven, we shall be fully living this supernatural life, which we shall know clearly. Meanwhile, on earth, our faculties of intelligence and will are raised by grace to supernatural acts toward God himself by the theological virtues.[22]

Virtues and gifts

The *Catechism* expresses this very clearly when it says that *the theological virtues of faith, hope, and love* "are infused by God into the souls of the faithful to make them capable of acting as his children and of meriting eternal life" (CCC 1813). And the *Catechism* continues, underlining the action of these theological virtues within man's psychological structure: "They are the pledge of the presence and action of the Holy Spirit in the faculties of the human being." Therefore these infused virtues have a precise aim: they "adapt man's faculties for participation in the divine nature".[23] They relate us directly to God: "They dispose Christians to live in a relationship with the Holy Trinity. They have the One and Triune God for their origin, motive, and object" (ibid.).

We have already seen the importance for the work of catechesis of affirming that we can truly know the mysteries of revelation, even though our knowledge remains a partial one; thanks to the virtue of *faith*, each of the baptized can have an intimate knowledge of God: "Faith is a filial adherence to God beyond what we feel and understand" (CCC 2609). We have also seen that it is vitally important to catechize in the light of our final goal, our end in God; thanks to the virtue of *hope* believers can move forward in their human and Christian vocations, desiring "the kingdom of heaven and eternal life as our happiness, placing our trust in Christ's promises and relying not on

---

[22] "All life is in motion and active", Fr. Marie-Eugene underlines. "All life has organs in order to develop, members in order to move, to act. Thus we have within us sensory life and intellectual life. Like all life within us, our supernatural life, our grace, also has its members, its powers of action. How does it tend toward its end, its term, Trinitarian life? Precisely through its activity, the activity of its members, its faculties" (*Where the Spirit Breathes*, p. 41).

[23] CCC 1812; cf. 2 Pet 1:4.

our own strength, but on the help of the grace of the Holy Spirit" (CCC 1817).

Moreover, hope "keeps man from discouragement; it sustains him during times of abandonment; it opens up his heart in expectation of eternal beatitude" (CCC 1818). Finally, we have noted that the work of *love* provides us with the source and goal of catechesis; thanks to the virtue of charity we can "love God above all things for his own sake, and our neighbor as ourselves for the love of God" (CCC 1822). Charity is the ruling virtue, "the perfect harmony" (Col 3:14); it is the source and the end of prayer, which "draws everything into the love by which we are loved in Christ and which enables us to respond to him by loving as he has loved us. Love is the source of prayer; whoever draws from it reaches the summit of prayer" (CCC 2658).

In these theological virtues we find both pedagogical principles and spiritual resources for the catechist. In the area of *pedagogy*, the theological virtues of faith, hope, and love are the key to providing us with a resolution of what is often described as a tension between teaching and practice, between "orthodoxy" and "orthopraxis". John Paul II spoke of this issue in *Catechesi Tradendae*: "It is useless to play off orthopraxis against orthodoxy: Christianity is inseparably both.... Revelation is not ... isolated from life or artificially juxtaposed to it" (CT 22).

An unhelpful debate can be undertaken between those who wish to emphasize a "doctrinal and systematic catechesis" and those who wish to concentrate upon "life experience". In the document quoted above, John Paul II was urging catechesis to avoid such polarizations. An understanding of the place of the theological virtues in the Christian life enables us to avoid this debate, for in these virtues we find the Christian *life* rooted in *glory*,[24] the glory of God and the glory of man fully alive in God. The theological virtues also reveal to us the *content* of Christian living, as answers to three questions:

- "Who am I?" Faith provides the answer.

- "What will become of me?" Hope can reach the answer.

[24] In Greek "doxa" means both "judgement" and "glory"; although "orthodoxy" is normally taken to mean holding a right judgement or view on a matter, we can think here of "orthodoxy" as "right teaching about glory".

■ "How am I to live?" Love supplies the answer.[25]

Fr. Marie-Eugene describes how our whole human being is raised by grace:

Faith is engrafted on the intellect, because the intellect has the power to know, or the power of intellection as the philosophers say. Grace too has its power to know, which is faith, and this faith is grafted on the intellect. Hope is grafted on the sensory powers. Charity, finally, the ruling power which impregnates all the others, an acting power, is grafted on the acting power of the soul which is the will or ruling faculty. Every human act is an act of the will. Every supernatural act implies an act of charity, the influence of charity. Thus, charity is grafted onto the will. In this way our entire human being is completed by grace and becomes divine. This is our treasure.[26]

Charity is the "ruling power", that which influences all that we do and all that we teach. By drawing our attention to its central place in our lives, the *Catechism* is helping to reinforce the centrality of love in our teaching.

Love is the central truth of the central mystery of the Faith, the mystery of the Holy Trinity, which is also, as we have seen, the source of all the other mysteries of the Faith. "God is love" (1 Jn 4:16). God is in himself an infinite movement of loving self-gift. The Father loves the Son eternally, and this love is received and returned by the Son. And that by which the Father and the Son love one another is himself a Person: the Spirit, the bond of love.

Love is also the central truth of the doctrine of creation; it is essentially a teaching about the overflowing nature of God's love. God does not keep being for himself but shares it through creation. He had no need to create; his creation is a gratuitous act. "God has no other reason for creating than his love and goodness" (CCC 293). As St. Thomas Aquinas put it, "Creatures came into existence when the key of love opened his hand." [27] Every moment of our lives is necessarily

---

[25] It is also worth noting that it is the Lord's Prayer that makes our theological virtues grow: "By the three first petitions [of the Lord's Prayer], we are strengthened in faith, filled with hope, and set aflame by charity" (CCC 2806).

[26] *Where the Spirit Breathes*, p. 42.

[27] St. Thomas Aquinas, In *Libros Sententiarum* II, prol.; cited in CCC 293.

an introduction to the love of God since every creature, all that is, exists because God holds it in being through his love (see CCC 27).

The doctrines of the Incarnation and the Redemption take up the incredible story of God's love. "The Word became flesh", the *Catechism* teaches, "*so that thus we might know God's love*" (CCC 458). That love was expressed, vindicated, and made available for us through the Son's Passion, death, and Resurrection.

The key doctrines that frame the Church's Faith, then, that give the Faith its fundamental form, the doctrines of God—creation, Incarnation, and Redemption—all richly express the implications of the truth that God is love.

What about other doctrines? Is love also central to them? What about our teaching on the Church? Well, we know her to be the Bride of Christ, being prepared for the eternal embrace of her Husband. The sacraments? Through them we receive "in increasing measure the treasures of the divine life and advance toward the perfection of charity".[28] The Christian life is itself ordered around the two great commandments of love of God and neighbor, of course, while the life of prayer, as we have seen, is "a cry of recognition and love", according to St. Thérèse of Lisieux.

It is not by chance that the Scriptures open and close with the account of a marriage (Gen 1:27; 2:20–25; Rev 21:1–3; 22:17). God's revelation of himself and his plan for creation begins with the marriage of the first human couple and it concludes with the marriage of the Lamb of God with his Bride. Love is the key to understanding the whole of God's revelation. This is why the Catechism speaks of the whole of the Christian life bearing "the mark of the spousal love of Christ and the Church" (CCC 1617). God has destined his creation to find its fulfillment in the closest possible union with him—a union that will not exclude the creaturely bonds we have, but transfigure them. In that union we will know and love even as we are presently known and loved by him. "God himself will be the goal of our desires; we shall contemplate him without end, love him without surfeit, praise him without weariness. This gift, this state, this act, like eternal life itself, will assuredly be common to all."[29]

---

[28] CCC 1212, citing Paul VI, apostolic constitution *Divinae Consortium naturae*; AAS 63 (1971) 657; cf. RCIA Introduction, 1–2.

[29] St. Augustine, *The City of God* (Harmondsworth: Penguin Books, 2004), 22:30.

Our relationship with God, then, is dependent on our acts of faith, hope, and love: we do not have other means to meet him. The *Catechism* also speaks of the gifts of the Holy Spirit. Baptismal grace gives us "the power to live and act under the prompting of the Holy Spirit through the gifts of the Holy Spirit" (CCC 1266). These gifts are "permanent dispositions which make man docile in following the promptings of the Holy Spirit" (CCC 1830). They can be compared to the sails by which a ship can move forward quickly, when the wind blows, instead of continuing to move slowly, thanks to the efforts of the rowers.

The *Catechism* adds that the gifts of the Holy Spirit "complete and perfect the virtues of those who receive them" (CCC 1831). This does *not* mean that, through these gifts, the direct influence of the Spirit in us supplants the acts of the virtues. The *Catechism* continues: "They make the faithful docile in readily obeying divine inspirations" (ibid.). These gifts allow the Holy Spirit to act directly in our human faculties, so that we are docile to him (Rom 8:14). For example, in prayer the Holy Spirit pacifies our intelligence or puts it in the darkness, and sustains our will, so that we prolong our act of faith in silence, or simply stay in an attitude of faith. The *Catechism* reminds us of the answer of a peasant of Ars who used to remain each day before the tabernacle. When asked, he told the Curé of Ars, St. John-Marie Vianney, "I look at him and he looks at me" (see CCC 2715).

What is the influence of grace with regard to the moral virtues, to those virtues which can be acquired by our own activity (see CCC 1804)? The *Catechism* here has some surprising affirmations, which we will do well to contemplate, and to lead others to marvel at: "The human virtues are rooted in the theological virtues" (CCC 1812). Courage, justice, wisdom, self-control—these human virtues are "rooted" in faith, hope, and love! We tend to imagine that grace crowns our human efforts, bringing a little extra to allow us to enter heaven. But this is not the case. For the baptized person, *everything comes from one's relationship with God*, which is lived out through acts of the theological virtues. "The theological virtues are the foundation of Christian moral activity; they animate it and give it its special character" (CCC 1813).

In case all of this sounds too "spiritual", we need to remember that *it is our whole human being, a creature raised by grace, which is acting*. We are one in being and one in action. Fr. Marie-Eugene insists on this unity of man sanctified by grace:

> Our journey toward God ... is not made solely through the activity of
> our supernatural powers, our baptismal grace. It is made by our whole
> being, our whole soul tending toward God. All our energies, even our
> sensory energies, have their part in it. It is a journey of divinized per-
> sons toward their end, toward the summit.[30]

We have spent a good deal of time examining baptismal grace and
the theological virtues and gifts that accompany it. Why is it so important for us, as catechists, to venture so deeply into the knowledge of
ourselves as an "organism of the Christian's supernatural life" (CCC
1266)?

- First of all, because *we need to realize* (that is, to *be aware of* and
  to *live out*) *our life as children of God,* and to take it into account
  in catechesis. Are we, and those whom we teach, really aware
  of what baptism means, of the supernatural means that are at a
  Christian's disposal and also the responsibility Christians have
  in growing as children of God?

- Second, because taking the time to explore the work of grace
  deeply is *essential for understanding and living a life of prayer,* which
  is mainly an activity of the theological virtues and an opening
  of one's heart to the action of the Spirit.

- Third, *because it is true.* As we have seen, the goal of catechesis
  is to become, in the Holy Spirit, the adopted children of the
  Father and thus heirs to his blessed life, in his Son and through
  him (see CCC 1). And this is not only a vague intention, an
  abstract idea, or a dream; it is the truth; it is reality.

The heart of prayer

The *Catechism* provides us with a rich text—not only biblically and
doctrinally, but also practically. It provides us with practical teachings
through which we can learn and teach how to pray. We have spoken
of the sources of prayer: the Word of God, the liturgy of the Church,
and baptismal grace. The *Catechism* also mentions

---

[30] Fr. Marie-Eugene, *Where the Spirit Breathes,* pp. 42–43.

- guides in the ways of prayer (CCC 2683–90, 2698);

- times for prayer (CCC 2659–60, 2697–98, 2742–43);

- places for prayer (CCC 2691);

- expressions of prayer: vocal, meditative, contemplative (CCC 2700–2724);

- the battle of prayer—against erroneous notions, failures, distraction, and so on (CCC 2725–58).

The prayer of the heart lies at the center of the Catechism's teaching on how to pray, and so this is where we shall focus our attention. "Composure of heart" is said to be the common trait of the different expressions of prayer (see CCC 2699). We must remember that the heart is not the seat of our affective life but of our deepest spiritual interiority (see CCC 2563). So recollection, composure, and the memory of the heart (see CCC 2697) lead to "dwelling in the presence of God" (CCC 2699).

In *vocal* prayer (which is the means of engaging both mind and body in prayer), the important thing is that "the heart should be present to him to whom we are speaking" (CCC 2700). Vocal prayer aims at becoming interior—not withdrawing into ourselves but turning toward the Lord.[31]

Meditation (which is a reflection on our life in the light of the gospel, mobilizing our thoughts, imagination, emotions, and desire) also tends toward union with Christ. At the same time, while "[t]his form of prayerful reflection is of great value, ... Christian prayer should go further: to the knowledge of the love of the Lord Jesus, to union with him" (CCC 2708). This prayer, in which "our attention is fixed on the Lord himself", whom we meet alone in "a close sharing between friends", is called "contemplative" prayer (CCC 2709).

The *Catechism* explicates the nature and the practicalities of *contemplative* prayer.[32] This type of prayer is not something reserved for monks or "mystics", nor is it an extraordinary state in the spiritual life. It is

---

[31] "Prayer is internalized to the extent that we become aware of him 'to whom we speak'", as Teresa of Avila says in the *Way of Perfection* (Rockford, Ill.: Tan Books, 1997), see chapter 26.

[32] Eleven paragraphs are devoted to it, in comparison with five to vocal prayer and four to meditation.

the essence of prayer arising from baptism as a new birth in Christ (see CCC 2718).

Instead of "contemplative prayer", which may frighten many, we could simply speak of "silent prayer" or the "prayer of the heart". Consider some of these beautiful descriptions of it: "Contemplative prayer is the prayer of the child of God, of the forgiven sinner who agrees to welcome the love by which he is loved and who wants to respond to it by loving even more";[33] "the simplest expression of the mystery of prayer"; "a *gift*, a grace", which "can be accepted only in humility and poverty"; "a *covenant* relationship established by God within our hearts" (cf. Jer 31:33); "a *communion* in which the Holy Trinity conforms man, the image of God, 'to his likeness'" (CCC 2713).

This prayer *is* silence, the "symbol of the world to come"[34] or "silent love".[35] It is "a *gaze* of faith, fixed on Jesus", which places us under the transforming light of God (CCC 2715); it bears fruit "to the extent that it consents to abide in the night of faith" (CCC 2719). It is a prayer of love and hope, of full trust in God, in "the obedience of faith, the unconditional acceptance of a servant, and the loving commitment of a child" (CCC 2716).

The *Catechism* teaches that undertaking this kind of prayer is always a question of a decision, of determination: "One cannot always meditate, but one can always enter into inner prayer, independently of the conditions of health, work, or emotional state. The heart is the place of this quest and encounter, in poverty and in faith (CCC 2710).

But this prayer is often difficult: the *Catechism* dedicates a whole article to the "battle of prayer". This does not only concern the decision to pray. It also concerns the troubles that we shall inevitably meet in the time of prayer. The only cure is a "humble vigilance of heart".

Thus we are brought back to the heart. In the distractions and dryness of prayer, we only have to go down into our hearts, into those deep regions of the soul where God is present and where we meet him by the theological virtue of faith, "beyond what we feel and understand" (CCC 2609). Inhabited by grace, our hearts are the source of

---

[33] CCC 2712; cf. Lk 7:36–50; 19:1–10.

[34] CCC 2717; cf. St. Isaac of Nineveh, *Tract. Myst.* 66.

[35] CCC 2717, citing St. John of the Cross, *Maxims and Counsels*, 53 in *The Collected Works of St. John of the Cross*, trans. K. Kavanaugh, O.C.D., and O. Rodriguez, O.C.D. (Washington, D.C.: Institute of Carmelite Studies, 1979), 678.

our filial trust, which rests "on God's action in history", that is, in the final instance, on the Passion and Resurrection of his Son (CCC 2738).

Catechesis as a school of prayer

More than anyone else, the catechist has to believe that prayer is fruitful for those who pray and for humanity: it is "a communion of love bearing Life for the multitude" (CCC 2719). Its main fruit is "the transformation of the praying heart" (CCC 2739). Animated by this filial trust, which is "founded on the prayer of the Spirit in us and on the faithful love of the Father who has given us his only Son",[36] even if it seems that we do not receive any answer in our silent prayer, we can make the perfect prayer of Jesus, who "prays in us and with us": "Since the heart of the Son seeks only what pleases the Father, how could the prayer of the children of adoption be centered on the gifts rather than the Giver?" (CCC 2740). United with him we receive the Spirit: "If our prayer is resolutely united with that of Jesus, in trust and boldness as children, we obtain all that we ask in his name, even more than any particular thing: the Holy Spirit himself, who contains all gifts" (CCC 2741).

The *Catechism* also underlines the fruit of prayer in the Christian life. It quotes the famous words of St. Alphonsus Liguori: "Those who pray are certainly saved; those who do not pray are certainly damned."[37] It insists on the fact that "prayer and *Christian life* are *inseparable*" (CCC 2745): "We pray as we live, because we live as we pray" (CCC 2725). Why? Because *love is a whole*: prayer and Christian life

> concern the same love and the same renunciation, proceeding from love; the same filial and loving conformity with the Father's plan of love; the same transforming union in the Holy Spirit who conforms us more and more to Christ Jesus; the same love for all men, the love with which Jesus has loved us.[38]

From all that we have been considering together, we can understand why and how catechesis has to be a "school of prayer": "The

---

[36] Ibid.; cf. Rom 10:12–13; 8:26–39.
[37] CCC 2744, citing St. Alphonsus Ligouri, *Del gran mezzo della preghiera*.
[38] CCC 2745.

catechesis of children, young people, and adults aims at teaching them to meditate on The Word of God in personal prayer, practicing it in liturgical prayer, and internalizing it at all times in order to bear fruit in a new life (CCC 2688).

This internalization in true prayer is the means of living personally the mystery of Christ that we confess and celebrate, so that it can bear fruits of holiness and conformity to Jesus Christ.

Praying is a human act: it has to be willed and learned. This is part of the mission of the Church, and primarily of catechists: "Through a living transmission (Sacred Tradition) within 'the believing and praying Church', the Holy Spirit teaches the children of God how to pray." [39]

In the silence of faith, prayer enables us to share in the "mystery": "In this silence, unbearable to the 'outer' man, the Father speaks to us his incarnate Word, who suffered, died, and rose; in this silence the Spirit of adoption enables us to share in the prayer of Jesus" (CCC 2717). Indeed, the "way of prayer" is to make us live concretely and personally the "mystery" of Christ: we pray to the Father, through the sacred humanity of Jesus, in the breath of the Holy Spirit, and in the communion of the Church, personified in the Blessed Virgin Mary (see CCC 2663–82).

With prayer we have a wonderful example of the development of Tradition through "the contemplation and study of believers" and also through their spiritual experience (CCC 2651). Prayer is a living knowledge that requires practice and experience. The *Catechism* has summarized for us this tradition of prayer in the Church, which has been handed on to us by so many saints, mystical doctors, orders and communities, and multitudes of unknown Christians. Each believer and every catechist is a member of this living Tradition.

Thus we can understand in which sense catechesis leads to a "loving knowledge of Christ" (CCC 429). It is not here a matter of an affective relation with Jesus. It concerns our personal relationship with Jesus Christ through the theological virtues of faith, hope, and charity, and the influence of the Spirit through the gift of wisdom. This produces a knowledge that is far more than affective or intellectual: it leads to the true "knowledge of God's mystery, of Christ" (Col 2:2; see 3:10).

---

[39] CCC 2650, quoting DV 8.

Here is the very goal of the Church's catechetical craft, as we can read *Catechesi Tradendae*: "The definitive aim of catechesis is to put people not only in touch but in communion, in intimacy, with Jesus Christ", and through him to "share in the life of the Holy Trinity." [40]

This loving knowledge makes both the catechist and the catechized not merely teachers but true witnesses as well, in words and in deeds. And in this way catechesis leads to evangelization: "From this loving knowledge of Christ springs the desire to proclaim him, to 'evangelize', and to lead others to the 'yes' of faith in Jesus Christ" (CCC 429).

And this in turn leads to a growing thirst for a deeper and even more precise knowledge of the truths of the Faith. The Second Vatican Council clearly expressed the importance of the gifts of the Spirit in the living Tradition—of which catechesis is a part: "To bring about an ever deeper understanding of revelation the same Holy Spirit constantly brings faith to completion by his gifts." [41] And the Council insists also on the importance of the life of prayer, together with study, for the development of this handing on of revelation:

> There is a growth in the understanding of the realities and the words which have been handed down. This happens through the contemplation and study made by believers, who treasure these things in their hearts (see Lk 2:19, 51) through a penetrating understanding of the spiritual realities which they experience. [42]

The scriptural references in this passage from Vatican II to our Lady are not accidental. As we have seen, the figure of Mary—from the Annunciation, where she receives the Word through her cooperation with the action of the Holy Spirit, through her pondering of that Word in her heart, her faithfulness to the Word even as she stands by the Cross, and her humble, grace-filled prayer that the Spirit at Pentecost would flood the Church with the capacity to receive and proclaim, in unity, that same Word—provides us with our living model of joy and hope as we ask the Lord to equip us to play our part in practicing the craft of catechesis in his Church.

And so we come to our final pedagogical key.

[40] CT 5.
[41] DV 5.
[42] DV 8.

KEY 12 PRAYERFUL

We make our catechesis a school of prayer, learning and teaching under the transforming work of grace.

Putting It All Together: The Twelve Keys

In practicing the craft of catechesis our catechesis is to be

KEY 1 HOLISTIC

We are attentive to the four dimensions of the Faith in our own formation and our catechesis.

KEY 2 GRACEFUL

In terms of the balance and relationship between the four dimensions of Christian faith and life, and their explication, we maintain the primacy of grace.

KEY 3 ORGANIC

We practice an organic reading and teaching of the Faith, especially through the use of cross-references in the *Catechism*.

KEY 4 PERSONAL

We are aware that doctrine and its transmission is essentially personal, and ground catechesis in the living foundational realities of the Faith, handing ourselves over to serve the transmission of Christ and his message.

KEY 5 TRUE

We proclaim the mysteries of the Faith as true, as realities that we can *truly* know, though never know *fully*.

KEY 6 ATTRACTIVE

We highlight the innately attractive nature of the Faith through using the beauty of nature and art and examples drawn from the joyful witness of those who have found their happiness in God.

KEY 7 PURPOSEFUL

We immerse doctrine within the *narratio*, the dynamic history of God's plan and purpose for our salvation, within which the "narrative" of every life can find its true meaning.

KEY 8 FAITHFUL

We select our key teaching points for any topic with the aid of the *Catechism*, alert to the specific needs of those we are catechizing, and fostering an ongoing learning "by heart", drawing on the language of Scripture and Tradition.

KEY 9 EVANGELIZING

We place our teaching points within the primary proclamation of the Faith, enabling a clearer understanding as well as a deepening conversion.

KEY 10 SCRIPTURAL

We let our catechesis be soaked in the Scriptures and "driven" by them, allowing the Holy Spirit to provide a spiritual understanding of the Word.

KEY 11 LITURGICAL

We teach so that those whom we are catechizing are led, in and through the liturgy, into a deeper understanding of, and participation in, the mystery.

KEY 12 PRAYERFUL

We make our catechesis a school of prayer, learning and teaching under the transforming work of grace.

BIBLIOGRAPHY

The main sources used for this study are, of course, the Holy Scriptures, the *Catechism of the Catholic Church*, and *The Documents of Vatican II*. In addition, we have found it useful to refer to other works at particular points:

Ambrosio, M. d'. "*Ressourcement* theology, aggiornamento and the hermeneutics of tradition". *Communio* 18 (Winter 1991).

Augustine. *De Catechizandis Rudibus*. London: Westminster, 1946.

———. *The City of God*. Harmondsworth: Penguin Books, 2004.

Basil the Great. *On the Holy Spirit*. New York: St. Vladimir's Seminary Press, 1980.

Belloc, H. *The Great Heresies*. Salem, N.H.: Ayer Company Publishers, 1938.

Brown, C., ed. *The New International Dictionary of New Testament Theology*. 3 vols. Milton Keynes: Paternoster Press, 1978.

Chesterton, G. K. *Orthodoxy*. London: Fontana Books, 1961.

Congar, Y. *The Meaning of Tradition*. San Francisco: Ignatius Press, 2004.

———. *A Messianic People*. Paris: Cerf, 1975.

Copenhaver, B. P., and C. B. Schmitt. *Renaissance Philosophy*. Oxford: Oxford University Press, 1992.

Corbon, J. "Maître, apprends-nous à prier: À propos de la Quatrième Partie du Catéchisme". In *Transmettre la Foi*. Toulouse: Éditions du Carmel, 1994.

———. *The Wellspring of Worship*. 2nd ed. San Francisco: Ignatius Press, 2005.

Dessain, C. *John Henry Newman*. Oxford: Oxford University Press, 1980.

Dix, G. *The Shape of the Liturgy*. London: Dacre Press, 1945.

Foster, K. *The Mind in Love: Dante's Philosophy.* Aquinas Papers 25. Oxford: Blackfriars, 1955.

Gallagher, J. *Soil for the Seed.* Great Wakering: McCrimmons, 2001.

Ghesquiere, T. "Bible-Reading and Liturgical Life". *Lumen Vitae,* 1955.

Gilson, E. *The Spirit of Medieval Philosophy.* Notre Dame: University of Notre Dame Press, 1990.

———. Introduction to *Grammar of Assent,* by John Henry Newman. New York: Doubleday, 1955.

Groome, T. *Christian Religious Education.* New York: Harper and Row, 1980.

Irenaeus of Lyons. *Adversus Haereses.* Mahwah, N.J.: Paulist Press, 1997.

John Paul II. *Catechesi Tradendae.* London: Catholic Truth Society, 1979.

———. *Fides et Ratio.* London: Catholic Truth Society, 1998.

———. *Redemptoris Missio.* London: Catholic Truth Society, 1990.

Johnson, P. *A History of Christianity.* Harmondsworth: Penguin Books, 1976.

Jungmann, J. *The Good News and Its Proclamation.* New York: Sadlier, 1961.

———. "Liturgy and the History of Salvation". *Lumen Vitae,* 1955.

Kavanaugh, A. *On Liturgical Theology.* Pueblo: Pueblo Publishing, 1994.

Kevane, E. *Jesus the Divine Teacher: Fullness and Mediator of Biblical Revelation.* New York: Vantage Press, 2003.

———. *Teaching the Catholic Faith Today.* New York: St. Paul Editions, 1982.

Knowles, D. *The Evolution of Medieval Thought.* 2nd ed. London: Longman, 1989.

Lewis, C. S. *Mere Christianity.* London: Fount, 1977.

Louf, A. *Teach Us to Pray.* London: Darton, Longman and Todd, 1974.

McGuire, B. *Friendship and Community: The Monastic Experience 350–1250.* Kalamazoo: Cistercian Publications, 1988.

MacIntyre, A. *After Virtue.* London: Duckworth, 1985.

Marie-Eugene of the Child Jesus, O.C.D. *I Want to See God.* New York: Resources for Christian Living, 1996.

————. *Where the Spirit Breathes: Prayer and Action*. New York: Alba House, 1998.

Marthalar, B. *The Catechism Yesterday and Today*. Collegeville: Liturgical Press, 1995.

Minto, A. "How the Divine Pedagogy Teaches". *The Sower*, October 2003, 6–8.

Newman, J. H. *Apologia pro vita sua*. Edited by W. Oddie. London: Dent, 1993.

————. *Development of Doctrine*. London: Sheed and Ward, 1954.

————. *An Essay in Aid of a Grammar of Assent*. Edited by I. T. Ker. Oxford: Clarendon Press, 1985.

Nozick, R. *Philosophical Explorations*. Oxford: Oxford University Press, 1981.

Pieper, J. *Guide to Thomas Aquinas*. San Francisco: Ignatius Press, 1991.

Pinckaers, S. "The Desire for Happiness as a Way to God". In *Thomas Aquinas: Approaches to Truth*, edited by James McEvoy and Michael Dunne. Dublin: Four Courts Press, 2002.

Pirenne, H. *A History of Europe from the Invasions to the XVI Century*. New York: University Books, 1955.

Pius XII. *Mediator Dei*. London: Catholic Truth Society, 1947.

Purcell, M. *The First Jesuit, Ignatius of Loyola*. Dublin: M. H. Gill and Son, 1956.

Ratzinger, J. *Gospel, Catechesis, Catechism*. San Francisco: Ignatius Press, 1997.

Roman Catechism. Translated by Eugene Kevane and R. Bradley. New York: St. Paul Editions, 1984.

Sacred Congregation for the Clergy, *General Catechetical Directory*. London: Catholic Truth Society, 1971.

Schönborn, C. "Address on 10th Anniversary of the publication of the Catechism", October 2002. Translated by D. Plunkett. *The Sower*, July 2003: 5–9.

————. "A Time of Desert for Theology: *Ressourcement* versus Models of the Church". *Houston Catholic Worker*, vol. 19, no. 7 (1999).

———, and J. Ratzinger. *Introduction to the Catechism of the Catholic Church.* San Francisco: Ignatius Press, 1994.

Schreck, A. *Vatican II: The Crisis and the Promise.* Cincinnati: Servant Books, 2005.

Sheed, F. *Are We Really Teaching Religion?* London: Sheed and Ward, 1953.

Sokolowski, R. *Introduction to Phenomenology.* Cambridge: Cambridge University Press, 1999.

Stern, K. *The Flight from Woman.* New York: Farrar, Straus and Giroux, Noonday Press, 1965.

Teresa of Avila. *The Way of Perfection.* Tan Books, 1997.

Thomas Aquinas. *Summa Theologica.* Translated by the Fathers of the English Dominican Province. London: Burns and Oates, 1922.

Traherne, T. *Centuries.* Oxford: Oxford University Press, 1960.

Vagaggini, C. *Theological Dimensions of the Liturgy.* London: Geoffrey Chapman, 1985.

Wallace-Hadrill, J. *The Frankish Church.* Oxford: Oxford University Press, 1983.

Walsh, M., ed. *Commentary on the Catechism.* London: Geoffrey Chapman, 1992.

Wojtyla, K. *Sources of Renewal.* London: HarperCollins, 1981.

Wrenn, M. *Catechisms and Controversies: Religious Education in the Postconciliar Years.* San Francisco: Ignatius Press, 1991.